The Five Senses of Romantic Love

Other Books by Sam Laing

Be Still My Soul: A Practical Guide to a
Deeper Relationship with God

The Guilty Soul's Guide to Grace:
Opening the Door to Freedom in Christ

Mighty Man of God: A Return to the
Glory of Manhood

Friends and Lovers: Marriage As God Designed It
coauthored with Geri Laing

Raising Awesome Kids in Troubled Times
coauthored with Geri Laing

The Wonder Years: Parenting Teens and Preteens
coauthored with Geri Laing and
Elizabeth Laing Thompson

The Five Senses of Romantic Love

GOD'S PLAN FOR EXCITING SEXUAL INTIMACY IN MARRIAGE

Sam Laing

DPI
DISCIPLESHIP
PUBLICATIONS
INTERNATIONAL

www.dpibooks.org

The Five Senses of Romantic Love
© 2008 by Discipleship Publications International
5016 Spedale Court #331
Spring Hill, TN 37174

All Scripture quotations, unless indicated, are taken from
the NEW INTERNATIONAL VERSION.
Copyright ©1973, 1978, 1984 by the
International Bible Society.
Used by permission of Zondervan Publishing House.
All rights reserved.

The "NIV" and "New International Version" trademarks
are registered in the United States Patent Trademark Office
by the International Bible Society.
Use of either trademark requires the permission of
the International Bible Society.

ISBN 10: 1-57782-223-4
ISBN 12: 978-1-57782-223-3

Cover Design: Brian Branch, Full Sercal Graphix
Interior Design: Thais Gloor

To my wife, Geri,

"...my darling, my beautiful one...
your voice is sweet,
and your form is lovely."

Place me like a seal over your heart,
　　like a seal on your arm;
for love is as strong as death,
　　its jealousy unyielding as the grave.
It burns like blazing fire,
　　like a mighty flame.
Many waters cannot quench love;
　　rivers cannot wash it away.
If one were to give
　all the wealth of his house for love,
it would be utterly scorned.

Song of Songs 8:6–7

Contents

The Absolutely Essential Must-Read Owner's Guide, Introduction and User's Manual to The Five Senses of Romantic Love

I got your attention with that chapter title, didn't I?

Yes I did, and for good reason. There are a few things to talk about before we just plunge into what we want to do. Let's go through some important items point by point.

First, this book is for married couples. If you are single, close this book *now* and go get your money back. No, wait! Better yet (for me, the author), keep it—but wrap it up and give it to a married friend. Or, maybe you can put it in one of those time capsules that you seal up, bury and break open in the future—in this case about twenty-four hours before your wedding day. Yes, the book is pretty explicit. Not by the tawdry conventions of modern sexual literature, mind you. But, by the standards of what godly single people ought to be reading, it's just not appropriate for you.

Second, this book, in spite of my humorous little

title of this introductory chapter, is not a "how to" manual. There are no steps to follow, no diagrams to study, no exercises to do. As a matter of fact, the worst thing you could do as a married man or woman is to look at this book as some sort of gauge that measures your sexual performance or a rule book that pressures you to adopt a certain type of sexual practice. Why is it that we as humans want to quantify and measure everything? Sexual love is far too wonderful a gift to be consigned to a "now do this" kind of program.

If you read this book and find yourself feeling any sort of pressure to do something that bothers your scruples or offends your conscience, or just doesn't appeal to you, then trust me, you misunderstand my intent. And, if you read this book and use it to beat up on your spouse with a "See there, I just knew all along you were wrong about that" kind of attitude, then you, too, have gotten off track.

And if at any point in your reading you are feeling overwhelmed, doubtful or discouraged, just turn over to the end of the book to the Afterword and read there to get the perspective you need.

So what are we hoping to do?

Here's what: *We are trying to take a look at how God sees sex in marriage and wrap our minds around it so we can experience as wedded couples the sexual joy and freedom he intends for us.*

How will we do this?

We will carry out this mission by studying what God says about it, specifically what he reveals in an oft-neglected, oft-misunderstood book in the Bible called the Song of Songs (or the Song of Solomon).

Third, *The Five Senses of Romantic Love* is written as an overview, an unveiling of the Song of Songs, and not as a scholarly commentary. While valuing and seeking to be true to the linguistic, cultural and theological insights of biblical scholarship, our purpose is to fulfill the purpose of the Song, which is to help us as married couples have a more fulfilling sex life. I certainly have attempted to be faithful to the text and hope that I have not been cavalier or careless in my exposition. In areas where there is room for varying interpretations (and there are many in the Song), I have tried to inform you, the reader, and guide you to the works of skilled, knowledgeable exegetes.

Fourth, in this volume we will work with the conviction that the Song of Songs is *not* an allegory of the love story of God and Israel, or of Christ and the church, as was believed by many ancient commentators—and a position that continued to hold sway into relatively recent history. Only in the last hundred years or so have interpreters gained the objectivity to let the book simply be what it is: a love story about a man and a woman. As I will elaborate upon in the next chapter, the unnatural allegorizing of the book may tell us more about the sexual and theological presuppositions of those who hold certain views than it does about the Song itself. And I say this with all due respect.

The truth is that all of us have on our tinted glasses—cultural, societal and historical lenses that affect how we read Scripture. It is not that we are all in a fog or that the Bible is inscrutable; it is just that we all are, well...human.

I wonder, what blinders might you and I be wearing? We are all in a search for truth. And while the Bible and the truth within it never changes, we have the obligation and challenge to look at the Scriptures with eyes unprejudiced by the "crooked generation" in which we live.

This brings us to point number five. The Song is describing the relationship of a man and his wife—*a married couple*—and not some sort of illicit affair. The five-fold use of the term "bride" and many other evidences in the text lead me and the majority of biblically conservative interpreters to this conclusion.[1] We can read this book knowing that the lovers are right with God, and that he approves and blesses their attitudes and activities.

As with everything God has designed, the plan works to its ultimate fulfillment when we let him take first place in our lives. The sexual relationship in marriage finds its richest delights with those who are united with Christ and depend upon his power to practice his unconditional love and generous grace.

---

1. See 4:8–12, 5:1 for the "bride" references.

Some folks wonder why God put the Song in the Good Book in the first place. It doesn't seem to them to fit in with the rest of the books in the Bible that deal with the weighty themes of creation, the fall, redemption and the like.

Ready for point number six? I believe this book is in the canon for a very simple, but profound and priceless reason: because God, in his love and grace, wants wedded couples—and all humanity for that matter—to know and understand just how great a gift he has given us in marital sexual love, and beyond that to experience that relationship with all five God-given senses.

And now for point seven. Who wrote this book, and who are the characters?

The book was either written by Solomon himself, or adopted and edited by him, just as he did with the book of Proverbs. As with other books of Scripture whose author or authors are not specifically identified, we can rest assured that behind the human hand was the divine inspiration of the Holy Spirit.

The characters? She is called "The Shullamite" (6:13), which is at best an obscure geographical reference, perhaps to her home town. Besides the opening identification in 1:1 as the book being "Solomon's Song of Songs," Solomon's name appears five more times in the text.[2] But a careful reading does not with absolute certainty identify King Solomon himself as the leading man in the story. Yes, the woman talks about the

---

2. See 1:5, 3:7, 9, 11; 8:11–12

"king," but is that Solomon or is it a generalized name referring to someone else?

The woman clearly calls the man her "lover" and her "darling," and he calls her his "beloved." I think that these terms may be the key to understanding who the characters are, and their significance: whoever they are—even if they are meant to be a generalized portrait of any husband or wife—they are with divine inspiration presented to inspire, inform and educate us.[3] If you wish to probe more deeply into this fascinating study, see the bibliography for a modest listing of commentaries that will help you in your journey.

Read the Song of Songs on your own. See what you think. Read it over and over again. Let its message begin to sink in. Just like every other book in God's Word, it has a message, one we need to hear, understand and absorb.

Wait a minute…I think I hear music playing. Do you? Are you ready? Let's get started!

---

3. Liberal scholarship would have us believe that many characters in the Bible were not real people, but legendary fabrications. To the contrary, when Scripture in historical narrative identifies its characters as "real life" people (such as David or Moses), we should take it at face value. Here in the Song, which is poetry, we are not dealing with a clear case of historical identification, but with a literary device.

Chapter 1

Holy and Hot

Let him kiss me with the kisses of his mouth—
for your love is more delightful than wine.
Song of Songs 1:2

"Let him kiss me with the kisses of his mouth."
Sounds a little like dialogue from a torrid romance
novel, doesn't it? Or, maybe a line from one of those x-
rated sexual enhancement manuals flooding the market
these days. We read these words and think they came
from the kind of book we would read with hesitation
and misgivings, and with the fear that we might be
found out.

Worse yet, we might even assume that these words
are the come-on of a loose woman, the sultry entice-
ment to a passionate, but illicit sexual liaison.

But the words above are not taken from a trashy
romance novel or a vulgar sex manual, nor are they the
alluring invitation of a woman of the night. No, these
words are the opening line of a book in the Bible—in
the *Old Testament,* mind you—and they are spoken by
a virtuous wife to her faithful husband, the man she

married and loves. And this is only the beginning—it just keeps on heating up! There is much more that this married couple have to say to each other about their sexual desires, feelings and experiences.

The title of this book in the Bible is the Song of Songs, or as it is sometimes called, the Song of Solomon.[1] Similar to the double appellation "Lord of Lords" given to Jesus—meaning that that he is the greatest of all Lords—so the title "Song of Songs" means that this song is the greatest of songs, or perhaps, the greatest of Solomon's songs.

Let's think about that for a minute. Whatever that title may precisely mean, we begin to get the idea that God, in his wisdom and love, has placed in the Bible a book devoted to telling us how exciting, adventurous and fulfilling sexual love in marriage can be—*and should be.*

God Says Sex Is Good

As we noted earlier, Song of Songs is found in the Old Testament. That's right, in the Old Testament—the first part of the Bible that some of us erroneously think of as the dusty, negative, rules-laden, joy-robbing volume; that part of the Bible written before Jesus came along and brought the good news. It is right in the middle of this Old Testament that God showed he is a life-

---

1. For our purposes in this work, we will often simply refer to it as the Song.

affirming Father who plans for his children to have zest and excitement in marriage.

Now let's be honest: most of us think that when it comes to sex, the Bible has nothing but warnings and condemnation. We have the notion that the Bible only identifies sex as the forbidden fruit, the tool of the devil, and the destroyer of our souls. At best, we may think that the Good Book permits sex for the practical purpose of procreation. The idea that married couples could or should have a passionate, delightful, adventurous, all-five-senses love life together seems, well…a little heretical.

And down through the ages the church has been one of the greatest culprits in perpetuating this notion. In failing to recognize and proclaim the beauty of God-given sexual pleasure in marriage, and in its one-sided preoccupation with the biblical prohibitions against sexual sin, the church has done us a great disservice. Let me say it straight up: this wrong-headed teaching is one of the greatest travesties ever foisted upon the human race by well-meaning, but misguided, churchmen and theologians.[2]

Even to bring up the subject of sexual enjoyment in marriage raises eyebrows and caution flags. Some think

2. Please forgive me for the broad swath I am cutting here. I know there are significant exceptions to my statement. Especially in recent years there have been a number of volumes written from a biblical perspective that celebrate our sexuality. And, I do not wish to be mean-spirited. It is just that I am passionate about the subject, if you get my meaning!

that such a discussion is outside the bounds of God's word and inappropriate for Christian people to talk about; that to address the topic is immodest, undignified and borderline unholy.

I beg to differ. *Furthermore, God, in the Bible, begs to differ.* If you want to learn from God about having a great sex life with your spouse (and who doesn't!), read the Song; understand what is really going on between these married lovers, and imitate their example. In the Song we have an unbeatable combination: the holiest *and* hottest sex manual ever written!

Warnings to Protect the Gift

Yes, there are plenty of warnings in the Bible about the abuse of sex. But we need to ask ourselves why they are there. These prohibitions are not in the Scriptures because sexual pleasure is innately wrong, dirty or selfish. Quite the opposite. It is because sex is such a wonderful gift that such ominous warnings are issued concerning its abuse. With its great potential for good, there is an accompanying possibility for evil if the gift of sex is used apart from the way God designed it.

Listen to this warning to young men from the book of Proverbs:

> For the lips of an adulteress drip honey,
>   and her speech is smoother than oil;

but in the end she is bitter as gall,
    sharp as a double-edged sword.
Her feet go down to death;
    her steps lead straight to the grave.
She gives no thought to the way of life;
    her paths are crooked, but she knows it not.

Now then, my sons, listen to me;
    do not turn aside from what I say.
Keep to a path far from her,
    do not go near the door of her house,
lest you give your best strength to others
    and your years to one who is cruel,
lest strangers feast on your wealth
    and your toil enrich another man's house.
At the end of your life you will groan,
    when your flesh and body are spent.
You will say, "How I hated discipline!
    How my heart spurned correction!
I would not obey my teachers
    or listen to my instructors.
I have come to the brink of utter ruin
    in the midst of the whole assembly."
(Proverbs 5:3–14)

Pretty scary, isn't it? We know what not to do. But what is the best defense against the illicit affair? What is the best reason not to give in?

Let's keep reading…

Drink water from your own cistern,
    running water from your own well.
Should your springs overflow in the streets,
    your streams of water in the public squares?
Let them be yours alone,
    never to be shared with strangers.
May your fountain be blessed,
    and may you rejoice in the wife of your youth.
A loving doe, a graceful deer—
    may her breasts satisfy you always,
    may you ever be captivated by her love.
Why be captivated, my son, by an adulteress?
    Why embrace the bosom of another man's wife?
(Proverbs 5:15–20, emphasis mine)

What is a husband's best defense against illicit sex? What is the compelling motive to stay faithful to his spouse? *It is the excitement and allure of lovemaking with his wife.* Look at the passage again and see what it is actually saying. The *breasts* of this man's wife were to "satisfy" him. The love of his wife—specifically, her *sexual* love—was to "captivate" him always (v19)"[3] This doesn't sound like boring, dutiful, mechanistic sex does it? It sounds like something thrilling, exciting, adventur-

---

3. A little elaboration on the words from the original Hebrew sheds even more light on the subject: "satisfy" means "to be saturated, to drink one's fill." The Hebrew verb *shagah* translated "captivated" may also be rendered as "exhilarated" (NASB) or "lost in her love" (CSB). It means "to swerve; to meander; to reel" as in drunkenness; it signifies a "staggering," expressing the ecstatic joy of a captivated lover. It can also mean "to be always intoxicated with her love." See *New English Translation* notes online: http://www.bible.org/netbible

ous, and as I mentioned earlier—with all holiness and reverence—something *hot*. And no little part of the reason for the heat is because this intense pleasure is to be utterly enjoyed without shame, with the full approval of our holy God.

Like everything else God made, we can use sex selfishly, outside the bounds of his will. When we do that, we sin. The greater, the more powerful and the better the gift, the greater potential for harm there is in its misuse. That is why Satan, our enemy, has taken sex away from God's purposes. Like everything else he lies about, he lies about this. He tells people that the best sex takes place outside of marriage. He tells people that the way to sexual fulfillment is one-night stands, or uncommitted relationships, or time-limited experiments with an escape clause. He tells us that married sex is at best routine, and at worst boring, and headed for obsolescence. And it seems there is some truth to his lies. Yes, the worst lie has an element of truth in it—but it is twisted truth, skewed truth, polluted truth.

Some people may have had some thrilling trysts and exciting encounters when they broke God's rules, but that doesn't tell the whole story. The fulfillment of our sexual needs and the answer to our sexual frustrations is found only within marriage. The story goes on beyond one night, one week, or even many years. The

story has to do with our long-term satisfaction, our permanent value as human beings, and our final standing
before God. Any other approach, no matter how
thrilling it may seem, just won't work out in the end.
That story ends in emptiness, heartbreak and disappointment...in this life and in the next.

Function Follows Form

God is a Father who loves us more than we can
know, and who made us with the capacities we have
for love and sexual pleasure. And certainly, God did not
make us with a sex drive so he could torture us or test
us. He made us this way in order to bless our lives; to
give us joy, fulfillment, excitement; and to experience a
loving union with our spouse

Think about it this way: in creation, function follows
form. That is, the Creator built our bodies in the way he
wanted them to function. We are given the drive of
hunger and the taste for food to motivate us to eat and
survive. We are given the reflex of breathing to supply
life-giving oxygen to our bodies. We are given the instinct
to socialize with others so that we may love and be
loved. And we are given a sexual drive so that we may
reproduce, to be sure, but also as a means, in marriage,
of satisfying our needs and bonding us to another person.

If, as some theologians contend, sexual union

between humans was only for the purpose of reproduction, it would seem logical to me that we should conceive children after just about every encounter. But as we know, this is not the case (thankfully!). The physical union of man and woman throughout their married lives serves even greater purposes: the expression of mutual love, the enjoyment of sexual pleasure, and the experiencing of closeness and bonding.

What we need is a radical—really radical—alteration of our view of God and his intentions for us. We need to revise our view of how he made our bodies and of the purposes he had in creating sexual desire within us. We need to come to a true biblical understanding. We can then revise how we look at sexual love and sexual pleasure in marriage. And when we do, the truth, as Jesus said, will set us free.

Total Freedom in Marriage

The Song starts out with the woman—yes, the woman—calling for the man to kiss her, and to kiss her repeatedly. She talks about his kisses being more delightful than wine, and in a later passage she says how his kisses glide over her lips and teeth. She invites him to kiss and explore her entire body. She says these things so clearly that it may astonish you, but they are unmistakably there.

Her husband, her "beloved," also says that her kisses are like wine, but he adds in rapturous, poetic language that her lips "drop sweetness as the honeycomb" and that "milk and honey are under her tongue." He says that the fragrance of her breath is like apples and her mouth is like the best wine. She responds to this by saying, "May my wine go straight to my lover, flowing over lips and teeth" (7:9).

Are you with me? Do you think we may be on to something here?

But that is just the start. There is more—much more—described in the pages of the Song. Their lovemaking is more intense, heated and intimate than kissing on the lips. Their entire bodies are involved. If this part shocks you, just hang on. Read the rest of the Song, and my brief exposition of it in this book, and you will see just how bold, exciting, excited and adventurous these married lovers really were. You will begin to see how they experienced and enjoyed their lovemaking with all five God-given senses.

It is the thesis of this book that sexual love in marriage is the hottest, best and most fulfilling and enjoyable sex on the planet. It is so because it was designed by our Creator to be so, and God just flat-out knows how to do things right.

Married couples need to claim the Song of Songs as their ultimate love manual, their own divinely-inspired romantic handbook. More than that, married couples need to make this book their emancipation proclamation—the claim of liberation from a limited, shy, tentative, simplistic, functional, boring sex life. We need to let this book do what God intended: *set us free*—free to enjoy sexual love with our spouse and free to experience a lifelong adventure of discovering each other's bodies, in all of their ever-changing intricacy and delight. God wants married couples to experience *as a lifestyle* the exciting, thrilling, adventurous and free sexual life that he, through the Holy Spirit, describes for us in this amazing book. If that is not why the Song is there, then why is it in the Bible at all?[4]

A Word of Caution

Remember that I do *not* intend to place pressure upon you or your spouse to perform sexually or to make either or both of you feel inadequate and guilty. Nor is my purpose to cause either one of you to compromise your conscience or your scruples. Those who

---

4. The most frequent interpretations of this book in earlier centuries allegorized it as a picture of the relationship of God to the nation of Israel, or of Christ to the church. The commentators were amazingly ingenious in finding spiritual applications to the sexual references in the text. While the relationship of Christ to the church will in the New Testament be compared to marriage (Ephesians 5), the Song with all its details about a man and a woman and their sensual experiences is, in my opinion, clearly about the delights of sexual expression.

are more adventurous must exercise loving and patient respect for their more modest mate; the more modest spouse should not judge the more adventurous one. Neither of you is "better" sexually than the other. The Song does not focus on performance, but upon love, encouragement and affection. The precise sexual activities and specific sexual results are left shrouded in mystery. This is the beauty of sex in marriage: God gives each couple their own pleasures and joys, and these are treasured between the two of you as a private, sacred gift from him.

This book is written to educate, enlighten and inspire, and to help us think more biblically. My purpose is to uphold a fresh and freeing ideal, and not to create a standard of performance. Some of you face physical and emotional difficulties due to health, past experiences, etc. We all find that as our bodies change, so our romantic life changes. Also, our love life changes as we grow in confidence and in closeness to our spouse. The beauty of God's plan is that each couple, in the privacy of our own marriage, has the freedom to decide for ourselves about our sexual intimacy, and have a lifetime to work out a growing and satisfying response to the teachings we find here.[5]

---

5. For more information about the sexual relationship in marriages affected by changes brought on by health problems or aging, I recommend *The Act of Marriage after 40* by Tim and Beverly LaHaye (Grand Rapids: Zondervan, 2000).

God's Plan Is Not the Problem

It is a sad truth that many married couples are sexually unfulfilled. The joy, pleasure and sheer delight designed for married men and women is, for them, the great unclaimed gift. And what is sadder yet is that, many *Christian* married couples are sexually unfulfilled as well. Most couples just accept this as normal. They subsist with a sex life that barely has a pulse, when they could be having the time of their lives in bed with each other—and for that matter, *out* of bed in other unlikely—and exciting—places as well.

What is saddest of all is that some married people have gone outside of their marriage, into pornography or adultery, in a futile attempt to find sexual fulfillment.

The problem is not marriage. The problem is not that God's plan is flawed. The problem is with us—with our ignorance, our unbelief and our low expectations. Though some married couples are not experiencing exciting or fulfilling sex in their marriage, that does not change what God says or promises—not one little bit. If we are not experiencing the promise, it is because something has gone wrong on our end of the bargain. We need to get educated so wc can see what we have been missing and also what we have been promised. And that is what this book is all about!

The good news is that "with God, all things are

possible." We can change. And when we change, our marriage changes. As Geri and I wrote in our earlier book about marriage, *Friends and Lovers*: "Any two people can change. Any marriage can be fixed. Any marriage can become great."[6]

And if you are a parent, one of the greatest gifts you can ever give your children is the example of your own exciting love life. Do you want your children to grow up and follow your footsteps of faith? Do you want to increase the chances of that happening? Have a great sex life. Your kids will see it (not literally!) and realize that the sexuality promoted out there in the world is bogus, and that they, if they do it God's way, can look forward to one day having a great sex life just like their parents have.

The purpose of this book is to help your marriage, especially your love life, become better than it has ever been. We will delve into the Song of Songs and mine it for its treasures—treasures that are meant to be ours and that every married couple is meant to enjoy. We will see how all five senses can be engaged in making love to your spouse.

Get ready for the ride of your life. Get ready to lose

---

6. Sam and Geri Laing, *Friends and Lovers* (Spring Hill, TN: DPI, 1996).

your confining inhibitions. Get ready to dismiss the
false idea that out there in the world, out there among
the glitterati, out there among those who disregard
God's plan—that "out there," outside the bounds of
marriage, is sexual joy and freedom, and that you and
your spouse are consigned *at best* to righteous, but
empty, sexual repetition. Throw out those false ideas
and claim what is yours—rightfully and righteously
yours—as a precious gift from your Father in Heaven.
Claim the joyous union of sexual love that your Creator
intends for you to have—a union he wants you to enjoy
and celebrate all of your married life.

The Song—your song—is waiting to be sung!

Chapter 2

The Sounds of Love

"Let me hear your voice;
for your voice is sweet."
Song of Songs 2:14

Words have immense power. They have the capacity to create and to destroy, to inspire or to discourage. What lovers say and hear is a defining characteristic of their romantic life. Words can resurrect a dead sex life, and can turn a routine love life into a sexual feast.

God not only uses words to describe, he uses words to create. And that is what the lovers in the Song do. They vividly describe and speak of their love, their attraction and their joy in their sexual union. But they also use their words to create their sexual life, to deepen it, to intensify it, to enhance it, to fill it with fire. We, like them, should use words to describe what we see and feel, and also to fashion what we wish to happen.[1] And so we too, by our words, build a sexual reality.

Words give sex its context, its meaning, its power.

---

1. This is a biblical and spiritual principle. See Mark 11:22–24. In this passage Jesus tells us to not only speak to God in prayer, but to speak our words of faith, intention and desire directly towards that which we wish to affect or change. (Also see Joshua 24:15b and 1 Samuel 17:32–50.)

They generate the atmosphere in which sex comes alive to its full glory. Without words, sex can be nothing more than a physical act and a vain attempt at physical gratification. With the words we speak to our lover, sex takes on meaning and increases infinitely in intensity and pleasure. For sex to thrive, it must be built upon and sustained by love, and that love needs to be expressed in words.

What are the kinds of words we need to speak and hear in order to have an intense and satisfying sexual life?

Words of Love, Commitment, Affection and Assurance

Throughout the Song, this husband and wife express their deep love for one another. Their fire of sexual desire burns brightly, and it burns because of the love they express in words. It is expressed repeatedly, constantly, effortlessly and in a variety of ways.

Twenty-seven times in this book the woman refers to her husband as her "beloved" or her "lover." Five times she says he is the one "my soul loves." The husband calls his wife "darling" nine times; his "bride" six times; his "sister" five times (this in his culture was a term of deep love and endearment); he calls her his "dove" three times, and, to top it off, his "perfect one" twice. Remarkably, of a total of 117 verses in the book, these terms of endearment, along with others not mentioned here, occur well over fifty times.

Many couples have special names and pet phrases for each other. Some of us once had them, but let them slip away. Resurrect the old terms, call each other those special names, and you will bring tenderness back into your marriage.

Men, do you want to increase the sexual pleasure in your marriage? Get closer to your wife. Increase the words of love. Remember that women are won, made happy and kept happy in marriage primarily by love and feelings of closeness. A woman's sexuality is brought alive by the intimacy of her friendship with her husband, and by the security of his love and respect. Your mutual sexual pleasure will flow from your relational connection, and that connection is built by *words*.

Words of Praise and Compliment

Both lovers are lavish and effusive in their expressions of praise for their partner's appearance. This concept is so crucial to the health of your love life that we will devote additional attention to it in the next chapter.

The man compliments his wife:

"How beautiful you are, my darling!
 Oh, how beautiful!
 Your eyes behind your veil are doves....
Your lips are like a scarlet ribbon;
 your mouth is lovely....
Your two breasts are like two fawns,
 like twin fawns of a gazelle
 that browse among the lilies....
All beautiful you are, my darling;
 there is no flaw in you." (Song of Songs 4:1, 3, 5, 7)

But consider also the wife's expression of her attraction to her husband:

My lover is radiant and ruddy,
 outstanding among ten thousand.
His head is purest gold;
 his hair is wavy
 and black as a raven.
His eyes are like doves
 by the water streams,
washed in milk,
 mounted like jewels.
His cheeks are like beds of spice
 yielding perfume.
His lips are like lilies
 dripping with myrrh.
His arms are rods of gold
 set with chrysolite.
His body is like polished ivory

decorated with sapphires.
His legs are pillars of marble
    set on bases of pure gold.
His appearance is like Lebanon,
    choice as its cedars.
His mouth is sweetness itself;
    he is altogether lovely.
This is my lover, this my friend,
    O daughters of Jerusalem. (Song of Songs 5:10–16)

Now let's admit it, most of us—men included—tend to be critical of our own appearance. And it doesn't help that we are subjected by advertising and the media to a ceaseless barrage of images of beautiful women and handsome men. We look at them; then we behold ourselves in a photo or in the mirror and wonder what our husband or wife could possibly see in us that excites them. And as the years go by, we increasingly focus on our flaws, bemoan our blemishes, and despair over our decline.

I say, let's declare war on Appearance Insecurity in our marriages! Let's become our spouse's cheerleader. Let's make it a habit to tell our partner every day, all the days of their life, that they still "have it." And when we do, we will help their confidence—and their sexual motivation—come alive.

Words of Desire

Sexual love in marriage has much to do with desire. Desire is wonderful, but fragile. How can we sustain and build it? The lovers in Song of Songs show us how: *Desire is kindled to a burning flame by words.* This couple knows that love's fire needs to be tended. It needs to be resupplied and continually infused with life-giving oxygen. In their lovemaking, words are the fuel that keeps the fire alive.

Listen to these words of desire spoken by the husband:

> "You have made my heart beat faster, my sister, my
>   bride;
>   you have made my heart beat faster
> with a single glance of your eyes,
>   with a single strand of your necklace."
>   (Song of Solomon 4:9, NASB)

He tells her that a mere glance of her eyes increases his pulse rate, and that when he looks at her decked out in her jewelry, his heart starts racing. What wife would not be moved by such a statement? We perhaps used to say things like this when we first married. They lit us up before—say the words, and light the fire again!

We may think that these kinds of desires and expressions are okay coming from men, but are not appropriate or to be expected from women. But the bride in the Song was no shrinking violet:

> My lover thrust his hand through the latch-opening;
> *my heart began to pound for him.*
> I arose to open for my lover,
> and my hands dripped with myrrh,
> my fingers with flowing myrrh,
> on the handles of the lock.
> (Song of Songs 5:4–5, emphasis mine)

> O daughters of Jerusalem, I charge you—
> if you find my lover,
> what will you tell him?
> *Tell him I am faint with love.*
> (Song of Songs 5:8, emphasis mine)

Her heart pounded with desire, and she wanted him to know it! This wife said to her girlfriends, "If you see my man, tell him I am lovesick for him. Let him know I want him so badly that I am feeling weak and faint." If your husband gets that message from you, it will send him through the roof. Has he been distant and unmotivated, and has he lost his desire for you? Speak to him your words of desire, and his mind will be on you the rest of the day.

Most men become sexually excited quicker than women. Wives, although this is a God-designed reality, it may frustrate your husband, who just does not understand why you are slower and less volatile than he. The solution to this frustration is not a reversal of roles, but is an issue of communication. Tell him when you desire him—even when you have only the first stirrings of those feelings. Understand that when you, the (usually) more sexually reticent, express desire for your husband, those words can ignite his feelings to a roaring flame.

You have the power to turn your husband on—use it and enjoy it. Isn't that part of your mystique, power and allure as a woman—the ability to drive your man wild? It is good, it is godly, it is fun—go for it!

Words of Invitation

As married lovers, our bodies belong to each other (1 Corinthians 7:4), and sexual love is an expectation, but we still need to *invite* each other to make love. Speak the words of sexual invitation. An invitation to have sex is an exciting thing! We should never take our partner for granted. We should never assume we can just walk in and possess him or her without some preliminaries. We need to ask. We also should not assume that our partner automatically knows when we are in the mood.

> Take me away with you—let us hurry!
>   Let the king bring me into his chambers.
> (Song of Songs 1:4)

Here this godly wife asks her husband to take her to the bedroom, and to be quick about it! Now let's break it down a little. She asks him to "take her"—she wants her man to be the initiator, in one sense, but she had the idea first! A kind of magical mutual leadership, if you will.

Wives, when you imitate this example, you will turn your husband's life into a paradise. You will win his heart, you will bring him joy, you will turn him on. Don't let false modesty and shyness inhibit you. Never think that initiating sex with your husband demeans or cheapens you. Far from it—it means that you believe in your worth and you know that your husband values you. It says that you love your husband and that you value yourself. Remember, you are his, he is yours—in body, in soul, in heart—as long as you both shall live. Have the confidence to initiate.

One of the wiles of the adulteress and the loose woman is her sexual aggression.

Women, allow me let you in on a secret: a sexually confident and aggressive woman is a real turn-on for a man.

If you issue this invitation in the morning, look out, you may make him late for work. If you call him at his work and invite him to join you in the bedroom later that day or that night, what is going to be on his mind the remainder of the day—other women? Forget about it! Wanting to hang out with the guys or stay late at work? You've got to be kidding! Will he be unmotivated, distant and self-consumed? Just wait and see!

She invites him to go away for some love in the country:

> Come, my lover, let us go to the countryside,
>   let us spend the night in the villages.
> Let us go early to the vineyards
>   to see if the vines have budded,
> if their blossoms have opened,
>   and if the pomegranates are in bloom—
>   there I will give you my love.
> The mandrakes send out their fragrance,
>   and at our door is every delicacy,
> both new and old,
>   that I have stored up for you, my lover.
> (Song of Songs 7:11–13)

But our lady is not done yet—she invites him in another way:

> Until the day breaks
>   and the shadows flee,
> turn, my lover,
>   and be like a gazelle
> or like a young stag
>   on the rugged hills. (Song of Songs 2:17)

What do you think these invitations mean? Well, what are gazelles and young stags like? You don't have to be a Bible scholar to know that these creatures are energetic, graceful and aggressive. The woman is inviting her lover to be fiery and assertive, to enthusiastically make love to her. Wives, is your man a little lethargic, a little lazy, a little unmotivated in bed? Try asking your husband to make love to you with some fire in his blood and see what happens. Women, if you ask for this, be prepared, you may get it! Not all lovemaking has to be this way; we need the leisurely, laid-back times as well. But, sometimes, regardless of our age, we need in our sex life some energy, some zeal, some passionate sweat!

> Awake, north wind,
>   and come, south wind!
> Blow on my garden,
>   that its fragrance may spread abroad.
> Let my lover come into his garden
>   and taste its choice fruits. (Song of Songs 4:16)

Okay, now her invitation goes from warm and enthusiastic to molten hot. What is she asking him to do here? She is calling him to possess her body, to touch, kiss and taste her in the most intimate ways, in the most intimate of areas. She longs for it, and she says so. She speaks with a dignified subtlety, but there is no doubt what she wants.

If he is going to really enjoy sex, a husband who deeply loves and respects his wife needs more than your *permission*—he needs your *invitation*. He needs to know that you, his wife, want him to touch, fondle, taste and caress you—all over. And he needs to know that your invitation is not reluctantly or grudgingly given.

A man who truly respects his wife often finds himself in a dilemma. He is desperately attracted to her and desires her body, but sometimes he may feel that certain areas are off limits. He may have some ideas about the kind of intimacy he wants to share with her, but does not want to be inappropriate or to violate her scruples or her conscience. He may find himself frustrated for this very reason—he longs for more, but at the same time does not want to be selfish. He is torn between his desires to be sexually free with her and to respect her wishes as well.

The solution? Part of it is to realize what this woman is really saying here, and to grasp that your Father in Heaven approves of it. Wives, God wants you to have a feminine aggression that you privately reveal to the man he has given you. There you can confidently give yourself—all of your body—to your husband to touch and kiss with no hesitation or qualms of conscience.

God is letting you know that you can and should ask
your husband to love and enjoy you fully.

Now it is the husband's turn to issue the invitations:

My lover spoke and said to me,
"Arise, my darling,
    my beautiful one, and come with me.
See! The winter is past;
    the rains are over and gone.
Flowers appear on the earth;
    the season of singing has come,
the cooing of doves
    is heard in our land.
The fig tree forms its early fruit;
    the blossoming vines spread their fragrance.
Arise, come, my darling;
    my beautiful one, come with me."
(Song of Songs 2:10–13)

First, using poetic and beautiful language, calling
her his darling and his beautiful one, he asks her to
come away with him. He asks her to arise. Is this a *double entendre*? Is he asking her not only to come away
with him on a romantic tryst, but also to let herself go,
to allow her desires to be aroused? Probably so. He is
asking for her to rise in her passions as well as to stop
what she is doing, go to a special place to be with him,
and make love.

"O my dove, in the clefts of the rock,
   In the secret place of the steep pathway,
Let me see your form,
   Let me hear your voice;
For your voice is sweet,
   And your form is lovely."
(Song of Solomon 2:14, NASB)

Men, there is a time to ask your wife to be with you and to make love to you. This husband asks his wife to show him her "face" (2:14, NIV) and to let him hear her voice. The NIV translation is unfortunate and limiting. Modern commentators translate the word to be "form," meaning "body" or "shape."[2] It is entirely appropriate for a husband to lovingly ask his wife to let him see her body, to unveil and reveal herself to him. Women, you need to know that your husband has a God-given desire to feast his eyes on you, and that it is not unmannerly, boorish or selfish for him to ask you for this privilege. Far from being inappropriate or insulting, it is a high compliment. Men, don't be afraid to ask, and women, don't be reluctant to comply!

Note that the word translated "voice" in the original language means "sound" as well as "voice." Now that certainly includes the spoken word, but the meaning is greater than that. Two verses previous we see the ref-

2. See Tremper Longman III, *Song of Songs: New International Commentary of the Old Testament* (Grand Rapids: Eerdmans, 2001), 123–124. Also see G. Lloyd Carr, *The Song of Solomon: Old Testament Commentaries*. Ed D. J. Wiseman (Downer's Grove, IL: IVP, 1984), 101.

erence to the "voice" of the turtledove. What is indicated is the intonation, the song, the distinctive sounds of the dove. The voice of the woman would be inclusive of any sound and intonation she makes. Okay, do I have to spell it out? Are the sounds you utter in lovemaking always actual words? No, no, a thousand times no! Sounds are…sounds. Don't be afraid to vocalize your pleasure, it will excite both of you. And, by the way, this is another reason that we sometimes need to be away in an especially private place for lovemaking. How can we freely vocalize if we are afraid the kids might hear? If you have been in the habit of being silent or subdued in lovemaking, maybe it is time to get out of the house, go to a secluded, private place, and make some noise!

And while we are talking about sound, let's not forget the power of music to set the mood and improve the intimacy of lovemaking.

> See! The winter is past;
>   the rains are over and gone.
> Flowers appear on the earth;
>   the season of singing has come,
> the cooing of doves
>   is heard in our land. (Song of Songs 2:11–12)

The right music can both relax and stimulate us.

Find out what music you both like, and enjoy it not only during times of intimacy, but throughout the day as well. God has given us a special gift in music, a treasure that has an inexplicable, almost magical power to create a mood and transform the atmosphere. Let's use that gift to grace our marriage, our home and our love life.

Words of Intention

> Your two breasts are like two fawns,
>   like twin fawns of a gazelle
>   that browse among the lilies.
> Until the day breaks
>   and the shadows flee,
> I will go to the mountain of myrrh
>   and to the hill of incense.
> All beautiful you are, my darling;
>   there is no flaw in you. (Song of Songs 4:5–7)

In these passages, the lovers express what they intend to do, what they intend to make happen.

The husband, after lavishly praising his wife's appearance, lets her know what he plans to do in response to it. He intends to enjoy what he has just observed and has just complimented. He does not just appreciate her breasts, he plans to enjoy them.

Later in the book, he becomes even more specific and graphic in his expression of intention:

How beautiful you are and how pleasing,
    O love, with your delights!
Your stature is like that of the palm,
    and your breasts like clusters of fruit.
I said, "I will climb the palm tree;
    I will take hold of its fruit."
May your breasts be like the clusters of the vine,
    the fragrance of your breath like apples,
    and your mouth like the best wine.
(Song of Songs 7:6–9)

He lets her know how beautiful she is, and after describing her as an elegant and graceful palm tree and her breasts as the attractive fruit, he tells her what he plans to do. He is going to climb that tree and take hold of that fruit! What a great way to say it! Sometimes it helps the woman to know what it is about her body that excites her lover, and what he plans to do. Surprise is great, but a verbal description may help her get ready and excited about what is coming. Anticipation may just be more than half the enjoyment of making love.

Now it is her turn:

Let us go early to the vineyards
    to see if the vines have budded,
if their blossoms have opened,
    and if the pomegranates are in bloom—

there I will give you my love.
The mandrakes send out their fragrance,
　　and at our door is every delicacy,
both new and old,
　　that *I have stored up for you,* my lover.
If only you were to me like a brother,
　　who was nursed at my mother's breasts!
Then, if I found you outside,
　　I would kiss you,
　　and no one would despise me.
I would lead you
　　and bring you to my mother's house—
　　she who has taught me.
I would give you spiced wine to drink,
　　the nectar of my pomegranates.
(Song of Songs 7:12–8:2 emphasis mine)

This alluring woman lets her man know that she plans to take him to her childhood home, and there give him a thrill. What is the nectar and spiced wine she plans to give him? Is it the kisses she will shower upon him? Is it the pleasure of her breasts? Is it the sweetness of her most intimate sexual places? The commentators say "all of the above." Women, sometimes you need to confidently decide in advance what you want to do to please your man, and let him know it. The anticipation will drive him wild, and give you both a night to remember.

Words of Satisfaction

Perhaps the best way to close this section is with the expressions of contentment and happiness that this couple shared at the conclusion of their union.

She says to him:

Your love is more delightful than wine.
(Song of Songs 1:2)

And he says to her:

How delightful is your love, my sister, my bride!
   How much more pleasing is your love than wine,
   and the fragrance of your perfume than any spice!
(Song of Songs 4:10)

I have come into my garden, my sister, my bride;
   I have gathered my myrrh with my spice.
I have eaten my honeycomb and my honey;
   I have drunk my wine and my milk.
(Song of Songs 5:1)

They let each other know how much they enjoyed their lovemaking. They verbalized it openly. To silently roll over and go to sleep after having sex is a big mistake, and very de-motivating for your partner. Always express your satisfaction and your appreciation. Even if a particular night is not the greatest you ever experienced, you can know that you in love were united with your spouse and that you enjoyed the experience of closeness. The great thing about married love is that it is always good— always good to be close to each other, always good to express our love and feel our spouse's love, and always good to know that when we wake up the next morning, the love of our life will be there beside us, to have and to hold, and to love again and again, for the rest of our lives together.

Married lovers, it is time to start using the sense of sound to build, repair and energize the romance in your marriage. It is time to leave our silence behind us and start talking—before, during and after making love. Speak a new world into existence—a world of intimacy, pleasure, delight, and ecstasy—a world you and your lover can inhabit and enjoy all the days—and nights— of your married life.

Chapter 3

The Sights of Love

Lover
> How beautiful you are, my darling!
> Oh, how beautiful!
> Your eyes are doves.

Beloved
> How handsome you are, my lover!
> Oh, how charming!
> And our bed is verdant.
>   Song of Songs 1:15–16

What we see has immense power to create sexual desire. The lovers in the Song feast their eyes on each other, and they like what they see. In the passage above the husband proclaims that his wife is beautiful, and she declares her husband handsome. This is only one of many such descriptions of the pleasure they take in each other's appearance.

Did you think your wife was beautiful when you married her? Did you think your man was handsome? Sure you did! In all likelihood, something in your future spouse's appearance—something special about them— drew you in the first place. Sex is indissolubly connected to our eyesight. We fill our eyes with the sight of our lover, and our desires come alive.

What about today? Do you still find your wife to be attractive? Do you still think that your husband is good-looking?

Who defines who, or what, is beautiful? Who makes that decision? *You do.* It is your own taste, your own opinion, that determines what is beautiful in your eyes. The Scriptures say that God "has made everything beautiful in its time" (Ecclesiastes 3:11). God has formed each one of us in our mother's womb, and to our loving Father, each one of his children is attractive. We may not be attractive to some people, or even to most people, but we are created in our Father's image, and that is good enough.

The glorious thing about marriage is that our spouse chose to marry us, knowing exactly what we looked like. I often joke that God temporarily blinded Geri during the years of our courtship, only to open her eyes to what I really looked like after she married me! But that is only a joke. When Geri saw me, she liked what she saw. As for me, I absolutely knew how I felt about her appearance the first time I saw her across a crowded room. And I have never changed my mind.

Yes, the years have their effect on our looks. Our hair may turn gray or disappear, our complexion may lose some its youthful hue, our skin may wrinkle and crinkle, but to us, the person we married is always the beautiful woman, the handsome man we fell in love with and pledged to be with to the end of our days.

That is the greatness and wisdom of God in designing marriage. It is not a commitment that has an expiring warranty or a trade-in clause as the equipment ages. How tragic, if the only people we considered to be attractive were the young. If so, life, and marriage, would be a slow descent into the abyss of a declining and disappearing glory.

Listen to the words of the husband as he describes his wife:

All beautiful you are, my darling;
    there is no flaw in you. (Song of Songs 4:7)

After reading this, we are tempted to say, "All right, buddy, stop your lying, and tell the truth. Do you really think your wife's appearance is *flawless*? I mean, even the supermodels have to be enhanced, improved and disguised a bit! Who are you kidding?"

The love lesson we learn from these words of the husband in the Song is one of the most important: *You decide and define for yourself and for your spouse just how beautiful or handsome they are.* It is your opinion of them that matters most to you, and to them. God did not make a mistake when he made your other half, and you like them just the way he made them! You are happy with the job he did. They are, and always will be, as Joshua Kadison sings, "beautiful in your eyes." We are bombarded daily with a message from the world, delivered on television, in the movies, and in advertising: *Here is the way you need to look. This thin. This young. This perfect. If you don't measure up, buy our product and improve your looks. Then you will be attractive and desirable to others. Then you can feel good about yourself.*

The message is so pervasive and persuasive that we accept it without even realizing it. And when we do, we are allowing others, with their warped values and money-driven motives, to define our lives for us. We don't even stop to think that the supermodels, movie stars and glitterati are airbrushed, surgically enhanced and dressed in fashion that no one wears or could wear 24/7 anyway. What do they look like when they get out of bed in the morning? What does she look like when she is changing a diaper, doing the laundry or cooking dinner? What does he look like when he mows the lawn, works on his car or plays with his kids? It is time for us to have a reality check, and to realize that most of what we see on the screen and in the magazines is just not real, and certainly not realistic.

Appreciate and Celebrate Uniqueness

> Sixty queens there may be,
>   and eighty concubines,
>   and virgins beyond number;
> but my dove, my perfect one, is unique.
> (Song of Songs 6:8–9a)

Husbands, do you know what is special about your wife? She is one of a kind. She is unique. And above all, she is yours.

If a wife believes that in her husband's eyes, she is beautiful, a great love life is possible. If a husband knows that when his wife looks at him, she sees a man to whom she is attracted, a lifetime of sexual joy is available.

We saw in the previous chapter how we needed to express in words our admiration of, and attraction to, our mate's body. Here we see again the ingenuity of God's plan in marriage: there is one person on earth whose opinion of our appearance matters most, and that person is married to us and loves us. They chose us, and we are theirs and they are ours. The pathway to a life of confidence about our appearance is now open and free for us to tread. Others can have their opinions. *So what?* Our culture may have its idealized picture of a handsome man or a beautiful woman. *Who cares if we don't match up to that?* In the private chambers of our own hearts and in the sacred intimacy of our sexual love, we behold each other with acceptance, awe, excitement and admiration.

Let's look for a moment at the descriptions these lovers give of each other's bodies:

First, the husband describes his wife:

How beautiful you are, my darling!
    Oh, how beautiful!
    Your eyes behind your veil are doves.
Your hair is like a flock of goats
    descending from Mount Gilead.
Your teeth are like a flock of sheep just shorn,
    coming up from the washing.
Each has its twin;
    not one of them is alone.
Your lips are like a scarlet ribbon;
    your mouth is lovely.
Your temples behind your veil
    are like the halves of a pomegranate.
Your neck is like the tower of David,
    built with elegance;
on it hang a thousand shields,
    all of them shields of warriors.
Your two breasts are like two fawns,
    like twin fawns of a gazelle
    that browse among the lilies.

Until the day breaks
   and the shadows flee,
I will go to the mountain of myrrh
   and to the hill of incense.
All beautiful you are, my darling;
   there is no flaw in you. (Song of Songs 4:1–7)

And then the wife describes her husband:

My lover is radiant and ruddy,
   outstanding among ten thousand.
His head is purest gold;
   his hair is wavy
   and black as a raven.
His eyes are like doves
   by the water streams,
washed in milk,
   mounted like jewels.
His cheeks are like beds of spice
   yielding perfume.
His lips are like lilies
   dripping with myrrh.
His arms are rods of gold
   set with chrysolite.
His body is like polished ivory
   decorated with sapphires.
His legs are pillars of marble
   set on bases of pure gold.
His appearance is like Lebanon,
   choice as its cedars.

His mouth is sweetness itself;
  he is altogether lovely.
This is my lover, this my friend,
  O daughters of Jerusalem. (Song of Songs 5:10–16)

It is significant to note the thoroughness of the descriptions these lovers articulate concerning each other's bodies. They both go from head to toe, and they leave nothing out: hair, temples, cheeks, nose, lips, teeth, neck, arms, hands, breasts, waistline (and the intimate areas near it), thighs, legs and feet. Our bodies are made in the image of God, and the human body—every inch of it—is reflective of his glory. As we learn to appreciate, admire and praise every part of our spouse's physique—both the intimately sexual areas and the other parts as well—it is then that we become truly and deeply sexually attracted and bonded to our partner.

What is it that you admire about your spouse's appearance? What was it that caught your eye when you first saw them? What was it that you began to notice as your relationship progressed? And, now that you are married and enjoy complete possession of each other's bodies, what are those features that excite and attract you? And if you say, "I don't think any particular area affects me that way," then realize that perhaps the years have blinded you and made you unappreciative. Seek to have a heart of gratitude. View your partner through eyes of love. You may need to pray for your eyes to open, or perhaps re-open, to see your spouse as desirable and endowed with all the indelible attractiveness that God placed within them. It is amazing what improvement in our spouse's looks may come with a change in *our* attitude!

Let's learn to be more admiring of our lover's entire body. As we learned in the previous chapter, let's let them know what those features are and what it is that lights us up. It may come as a surprise to your spouse to hear what it is that you admire about them, but knowing this will make them more sexually confident and alive.

The Beautiful Wife

But it gets a little more heated and little more specific than what we have seen so far as the husband says:

> "How beautiful are your feet in sandals,
>   O prince's daughter!
>   The curves of your hips are like jewels,
>   The work of the hands of an artist.
> "Your navel is like a round goblet
>   Which never lacks mixed wine;
>   Your belly is like a heap of wheat
>   Fenced about with lilies.
> "Your two breasts are like two fawns,
>   Twins of a gazelle." (Song of Solomon 7:1–3, NASB)

While it is difficult to know precisely what the man is describing in the words above, I have found a remarkable unity among the scholars indicating that he is, in delicate, understated, yet forthright language, describing some of his wife's most intimate features. The "navel" and "belly" are believed by students of the language to refer to the most private sexual areas.[1] I think his descriptions of her sexual features are as beautiful, romantic and exciting as they are complimentary. His poetic, rhapsodic language expresses his fascination and arousal and gives honor to the entirety of her divinely given beauty without a hint of demeaning vulgarity.

> "O my dove, in the clefts of the rock,
>   In the secret place of the steep pathway,
>   Let me see your form,
>   Let me hear your voice;
>   For your voice is sweet,
>   And your form is lovely."
> (Song of Solomon 2:14, NASB)

The husband here asks his beloved to let him see her "form." This word is rendered as "face" by some translators, but the more literal translation "form," indicating a broader reference to her entire body, seems to be more in line with the context and with the message

---

1. Carr, *The Song of Solomon*, 157–158. Also see Longman, *Song of Songs*, 194–195.

of the Song (as mentioned in the previous chapter). Most men will readily identify with this statement, and with this sentiment. They long to see their wife unclothed.

Wives, have you noticed that your husband will stop whatever he is doing to get a glimpse of your body? If you are having an argument and in the middle of it you happen to change your clothes, he will completely lose his train of thought. He will wander into the bathroom while you are bathing just to get a look at you. Rather than resenting this as juvenile and boorish, come to appreciate that the sight of your unclothed form is one of the greatest pleasures and joys your husband has in his life. And, know this: if he has been feasting his eyes on you, other women he sees in the course of the day will have far less appeal to him.

God has declared that in marriage we are one flesh (Genesis 2). In the Garden of Eden, innocent Adam and Eve "were both naked and were not ashamed" (Genesis 2:25). The Scriptures also teach us that "the wife does not have authority over her own body, but the husband does; and likewise also the husband does not have authority over his own body, but the wife does" (1 Corinthians 7:4).

If these verses mean anything, they mean that a husband and wife should be comfortable and happy with their partner seeing them undressed. In marriage, all the clothes come off and we see each other "as we are." In our counseling Geri and I have had to help some women who had a false sense of modesty about being naked in the presence of their husbands. Understand this: your body is a thing of honor, dignity and beauty. Your husband longs and needs to see you, and you need to enjoy it when he does. There is a time for being coy, a time for a little godly flirting, a time for you to tease him by concealing yourself. But, that is all for the purpose of ending up somewhere else—just like Eve in the garden! That is not to say that candles and muted lighting aren't appropriate, but nonetheless, let's embrace the fact that the joy of married love means that we can be unclothed and unashamed in the presence of our spouse.

If you feel you are unattractive and are not proud of your appearance, do what you can to improve, but don't allow your own overcritical attitude to prevent your spouse from enjoying taking you in with their eyes. Sight is important!

The Handsome Husband

We have spent a lot of our time talking about the beauty of the bride, but what about the handsomeness of the husband? Sometimes we think that care for appearance is the sole domain of women, and that men can ignore or neglect their grooming, dress and hygiene. The bride in the Song begs to differ—and so does your wife! She notices every feature of her husband's anatomy, just as he does hers. What she sees attracts her and arouses her desire.

Men, this tells us that we need to take care of ourselves, that we need to respect both our own bodies and the sensibilities of our wives. We need to groom ourselves and practice good hygiene (more on this in chapter 8). We need to dress in a manner that pleases our wives. Some of us have an eye for what makes us look our best; others of us dress in a manner that highlights our every flaw. Let your wife help you out here. Listen to her suggestions about what pleases and attracts her. I even listen to my kids when they lovingly warn me: "Uh, Dad, like, really, like, you just like, *totally* don't want to go out of the house in what you are wearing right now."

Men, let's not become sedentary, but let's stay active, alive and vibrant. Let's improve that diet and lose a few pounds. We will feel better about ourselves—more masculine and confident. Our bodies are a gift from God and are the temple of the Holy Spirit (1 Corinthians 6:19–20). While we never want to give primary focus to our exterior appearance, especially to the neglect of our inner selves, we must remember that our bodies belong to God, *and to our spouse.* Is it not a sign of taking one another for granted if we "let ourselves go" after we are married? Let our demise and decline come about due to the inevitable passage of time, not because of our neglect. For the glory of God, for the sake of living a long and useful life, and for the happiness of our wives and the enhancement of our love lives, let's take care of ourselves!

Clothing

> How beautiful you are, my darling!
>   Oh, how beautiful!
>   Your eyes behind your veil are doves.
> (Song of Songs 4:1a)

> "How beautiful are your feet in sandals,
> O prince's daughter!" (Song of Solomon 7:1, NASB)

The apparel we choose to wear makes a difference in our love life. While not as much is said about clothing in the Song as is said about the physical attributes of the lovers, apparel is mentioned and is significant.

Beauty concealed can be as exciting as beauty revealed. It is the glimpse of the woman's eyes behind or just above her veil that awakens the lover's desires and draws him to her. His wife's body, modestly but alluringly revealed, excites and arouses him to want to see her even more.

A woman who takes care to attire herself attractively for her normal activities will enhance her husband's desire. Most of us, in our days of courtship, were very concerned with how we looked. We bought clothes, borrowed clothes and changed clothes, all to please our sweetheart. Why is it that once we have won our mate, we can begin to neglect our appearance? While the demands of practicality make it impossible for us to always be nicely dressed and neatly groomed around our spouse, we should nonetheless maintain a deep respect for how we look.

Husbands, this means that you will need to sensitively provide your wife with the resources she needs to buy fashionable and attractive clothing. Do not complain about her appearance if you are not willing to invest in it. Women need more maintenance than men do—and for good reason: they are better looking than we are! I am not counseling a slavish devotion to fashion, but instead a wise investment in your wife's beauty and appearance. She will be all the more confident for it, and you, my friend, get to look at her every day! Remember, a nice hairstyle may cost something, but she wears it daily for several weeks. The same principle holds true for her nails and makeup as well.

Intimate apparel is worth the investment. Actually, I am a bit of a wastrel when it comes to this item in our budget. When Geri and I walk by the "unmentionables" store in the mall, I point her in the right direction, hand her my wallet, and invite her to empty its contents in a shopping spree!

Husbands, let her pick out her own items, with some of your suggestions and choices made here and there. But be careful, or your different tastes in intimate apparel can result in some intimate disagreements.

Wives, whatever you do, please do better than "Evening Wear by Nuns." Throw out your faded flannel gowns that go down to the ankles, button up to the wrists, and cinch up around the neck.

Men, let's get something a little more exciting for bedtime than our old gym clothes and high school boxers. Surely spouses can agree on evening wear that makes her feel attractive and feminine, and that makes him feel attracted and excited! Yes, wives, that sexy ensemble your husband loves may be unsuitable for comfortable sleep or a cold winter's night, but remember, it usually doesn't stay on for long, and after it has served its purpose, you can change into something more practical.

Cosmetics

> Your lips are like a scarlet ribbon;
>   your mouth is lovely. (Song of Songs 4:3)

Here the husband notices his wife's scarlet lips. This is most likely a reference to the enhancement provided by lipstick, since makeup was common in the ancient near east.[2] There is nothing inherently ungodly or unspiritual about a woman wearing makeup. Peter warns of the danger of overdoing it, especially when the inner life is neglected,[3] but his warning should not be pressed beyond its meaning. Peter cautions against surrounding a shallow, godless heart with a carefully appareled, manicured and coiffed body. It is a matter of having the right priorities. If the inner woman is harsh, arrogant and selfish, these traits will negate outer beauty, no matter how much effort goes into its cultivation.

Surely the examples of Sarah, who remained attractive even in her latter years, of the winsome and beautiful Abigail, and of the energetic and vibrant Rachel, tell us that proper attention to the feminine heart does not mean a commensurate neglect of the outer woman.

The wearing of makeup is a very personal decision and is a matter of taste. Wives, feel free to use cosmetics,

---

2. Carr, *The Song of Solomon,* 116.

3. 1 Peter 3:3–4

and find out what your husband likes.[4] Your makeup can stimulate his desire for you. It can also affect how you feel about yourself, and that makes all the difference in your sexual motivation. And find out whether he prefers you to wear makeup as you prepare for an evening of love. If he does, wear it, and get ready to have it rearranged a little!

Jewelry

> "You have made my heart beat faster, my sister, my
>   bride;
>   You have made my heart beat faster with a single
>   glance of your eyes,
>   With a single strand of your necklace."
> (Song of Solomon 4:9, NASB)

He tells her that she looks attractive and sexy in her jewelry. Now what does this have to do with lovemaking? Everything! He took one look at her decked out in her jewelry, and his heart started racing. What wife would not be moved by such a statement—what will happen to her heart rate? Women need to feel pretty in order to be sexually aroused, and nothing helps a woman feel prettier than jewelry. Yes it costs, but how much is she worth to you, husbands?

---

4. Some husbands prefer their wives to wear makeup; others do not. What matters is that both of you are pleased.

Your cheeks are beautiful with earrings,
   your neck with strings of jewels.
We will make you earrings of gold,
   studded with silver. (Song of Songs 1:10–11)

The husband tells his wife he intends to give her a pair of gold and silver earrings. Men, give your wife gifts that enhance her appearance. Sometimes they need to cost you something. Expensive gifts are not necessarily materialistic. No, the costly gift says, "I don't want to just be practical; I want to be lavish. I want to give you something precious, something valuable, because you are beyond price to me." The first significant gift most of us men gave our wives was an engagement ring. That ring said to her, "You are precious. You deserve to be decked in jewels. Here is a gift that shows how valued you are, that shows how permanent my love is, and that shows everyone that you are mine."

When Geri and I were about to be engaged, we went to the jewelry store to look at rings. We narrowed it down to two. She liked them both, but the one that made her eyes sparkle cost a couple of hundred dollars more. I so much wanted her to have the one she really loved, but I was working for the church as an intern and didn't make very much money. With the cost of the wedding, the honeymoon, and setting up our apartment, I felt nervous about spending too much.

A few weeks later I drove my 1969 VW back to the jewelry store to make the purchase. I parked at the front entrance and sat in the car agonizing over the decision. I thought about being practical, but I couldn't get the smile that came over Geri's face when she looked at that second ring out of my mind. I said to myself, "This is the person you love more than anyone else on earth. You've just got to get her that ring." Quickly, before I could change my mind, I jumped out of the car, locked the door and slammed it shut...with my keys still in the ignition!

The beautiful and costly gift makes your wife feel loved. It speaks volumes to her, and to others as well. Show me a woman whose husband gives her thoughtful gifts, and I will show you a woman who in all likelihood is very secure in her husband's love. Her confidence enhances her desires and inspires her to lovingly give her husband the most precious gift she has to give: her own body.

Environment

Beloved
> Take me away with you—let us hurry!
>> Let the king bring me into his chambers.

Friends
> We rejoice and delight in you;
>> we will praise your love more than wine.

Beloved
   How right they are to adore you!
(Song of Songs 1:4)

Our romantic life is greatly influenced by the environment we see around us. Let's start with the bedroom. It should be a sanctuary devoted to our intimacy and to our relationship, a place of beauty and privacy. Walking into a room that is littered with unpaid bills, children's toys and dirty laundry may indeed make our hearts begin to pound…but for all the wrong reasons!

Sadly, the master bedroom is often the most neglected room in the house. We may lavish attention on the living and dining areas and pour our creative efforts into the baby's or the kids' rooms, but we relegate our own bedroom to last place on our list, and it has the worst furniture in the house. We reason that since others are least likely to see it, we can invest less time in making it attractive. This attitude may just be saying something about our priorities, and about our understanding of the importance of our intimate relationship with our spouse.

Our bedroom should be a place of particular beauty because of the unique role it plays. It is worth the time and resources needed to make it special and attractive. Men, we need to give our wives the reins here. Most women find that a pleasant ambience helps them to be more at ease and romantically inclined. The right colors, tasteful decor, carefully coordinated bedclothes and fluffy pillows, flowers and the like all help your wife to relax, clear her mind, and to feel sexy and "in the mood."

If you have made your bedroom the trophy room for your ten-point buck, your mounted prize bass, or the display case for your high-school athletic trophies, be prepared for your sex life to suffer, unless your wife is just as sports-crazy and outdoorsy as you are.

The same may be true if you have let it become your personal office or computer workroom. Nothing douses the spark of romance more quickly than the constant reminder of work and a computerized voice shouting "You've got mail!" from across the room. I realize that there is leeway for personal tastes here and that some of us have smaller apartments. But the fact remains that what we see (and hear!) affects our mood.

The bedroom is the private domain of the man and woman of the house. Let us view it as our sanctuary, our place of escape, our place of intimate rendezvous. Let us maintain the sanctity of our bedrooms as our place of rest and of romantic love. The investment will pay enormous dividends in our intimate relations—not to mention our peace of mind.

"How handsome you are, my beloved,
  And so pleasant!
  Indeed, our couch is luxuriant!"
(Song of Solomon 1:16, NASB)

A good bed is a great investment. When Geri and I got married, we could afford very little furniture. We had a folding card table which served as our dining table, and the stand for our small black-and-white TV was a cardboard box Geri covered with contact paper. Friends loaned us some of their extra stuff. But we did wisely spend some money on one item of furniture: a nice bed. I tried to pay it off with one of those 90-day no-interest deals, but I ended up having to finance the last payment anyway. Of course we spent lots of time sleeping in it, but as newlyweds we used it for other things as well… I think that decision said something about the priority we put on rest and on love in our marriage, and we never regretted it.

And, while we are talking about the bedroom, let's remember to make it a place of privacy. We need a sense of security knowing that the windows are curtained from prying eyes, and that the door is locked. We cannot enjoy an uninhibited, relaxed romantic life if we feel our most private moments are in danger of being seen—or interrupted!—by our neighbors or our children.

༄

Let's close our thoughts in this chapter by going back to what we said at the beginning. Beauty is in the eye of the beholder. Wife, you married him, among other reasons, because there was something about him you liked to look at. Husband, you chose your bride because, among other reasons, she caught, and held, your eye.

Let us never forget these truths, and always have eyes only for the one to whom we pledged our life and love. And let's respect ourselves and our partner enough to do our best to look our best—inside and out.

Chapter 4

The Fragrance of Love

Pleasing is the fragrance of your perfumes;
    your name is like perfume poured out.
    No wonder the maidens love you!
Song of Songs 1:3

How delightful is your love, my sister, my bride!
    How much more pleasing is your love than wine,
    and the fragrance of your perfume than any spice!
Song of Songs 4:10

Fragrance just might be the secret weapon of love-making. Throughout the Song of Songs, both lovers repeatedly mention the arousing fragrance of their partner and their surroundings.[1] The Song goes on to depict their lively attraction to each other because of their wise and loving use of aroma. They used it generously, they paid the price for the expensive stuff, and they poured it on. They perfumed their bed, their garments and their bodies. They carefully prepared their most intimate areas for contact. An inspiring sexual life was the reward.

---

1. Its presence in the Song is ubiquitous, occurring at least fifteen times and in all but one chapter. Here is a short list: 1:3, 12; 2:13; 3:6; 4:6, 10, 11, 14, 16; 5:1, 13; 6:2; 7:8, 13; 8:14

Has your love life gone stale and become routine? It may be that fragrance is the missing element. Perhaps a refreshing breeze of cleanliness, care and fragrance will help turn things around.

The Power of Fragrance

What exactly is it about the sense of smell that has such an intoxicating influence on sexual love?

Fragrance is arousing.

> While the king was at his table,
>   my perfume spread its fragrance.
> (Song of Songs 1:12–13)

The woman in the Song uses her perfume deliberately to arouse the interest and desires of her lover, and she uses it with sufficient strength for him to catch her fragrance at the dinner table. When he breathed the scent of her perfumes, it got his attention, causing him to notice her. The senses of smell and sight work together. The king has already become aware of her fragrance, but he also looks upon her and sees her beauty.

> How beautiful you are, my darling!
>   Oh, how beautiful!

Your eyes are doves. (Song of Songs 1:15)

Are we beginning to catch the scent? Not only does the Song show us that fragrance is important in love-making, but it indicates that for *both men and women* the use of cologne and perfume can intensify the excitement in an encounter of love.

Some husbands think that men's cologne is, at best, a luxury, and at worst, a sign of weakness and effeminacy. Wrong! Men, don't make the mistake of dismissing fragrance as an essential for arousing your wife. The woman in the Song is representative of her gender—women love to catch the aroma of a masculine cologne. It could be that your neglect of this vital element is putting a damper on your wife's desire for you. Ask her what cologne she likes on you, start using it regularly, and see what happens. My bet is that you will start getting her attention, inspiring her compliments, and helping her get in the mood with far less effort than in the past.

Fragrance sends a message.

Its message may be subtle, but it is powerful and unmistakable. Fragrance denotes courtesy, sensitivity and respect. But in marriage, it goes even further: it tells our lover that we are ready for romance. Its presence tells our partner that we have been thinking about love, and that we are ready for an encounter. It says that we care enough about our spouse not merely to be inoffensive, but to be appealing.

Fragrance creates the proper mood for love.

The atmosphere of attraction needs to be carefully nurtured. Sexual desire is a delicate emotion. And something so fragile can be easily broken. The right fragrance builds that feeling, and the wrong one tears it down—and quickly. Lovemaking involves intimate physical contact. The careful use of fragrance makes every part of the body attractive. As much as the right fragrance is arousing, offensive odors are a deadly turnoff. Let's be sensitive to the power of fragrance for good or ill, and always strive to smell our very best for our lover.

Fragrance is an enhancer and an intensifier.

It makes the usual unusual. It makes the mundane exciting. Fragrance does more than just arouse your partner—it arouses you as well. It makes our bodies and our presence into an occasion of interest and arousal. Sex can become a routine physical act, or it can be an occasion of love and of passionate desire. Perhaps, in the context of lovemaking, no other sense is as powerful as the sense of smell in progressing from mere sexual interest to full erotic arousal. Perhaps no other sensation does more to bring the element of intense emotion and even athletic activity into our lovemaking.

You may think that as far as aroma goes, neutral or natural is okay. Think again. We are created in God's image, and he cares about scent. In the Old Testament, God caught the sweet-smelling fragrance of the incense of the offering and was pleased. The high priest was anointed with sweet-smelling oil before entering the presence of God, and carried with him an aromatic censer. Paul says that the saints are the aroma of Christ and are to spread the fragrance of the knowledge of God. In the book of Revelation, the prayers of the saints are regarded as incense rising up to heaven.[2] Scent changes the atmosphere, and makes it better. It matters to God, and it matters a great deal in our love life as well.

Fragrance brings sexual freedom and confidence.

Sexual freedom comes when we are confident that we are attractive and desirable. When our body is fresh, clean and sweet-smelling, we feel free to make our most intimate areas available to our partner. Likewise, when our partner is intoxicatingly anointed, we feel

2. Exodus 30:1–31:11; Leviticus 16:11–13, 21:10; 2 Corinthians 2:14–16; Revelation 5:8

free, with equal confidence, to explore, caress, touch and taste them as well.

The Variety and Value of Fragrance

> How delightful is your love, my sister, my bride!
>   How much more pleasing is your love than wine,
>   and the fragrance of your perfume than any spice!
> Your lips drop sweetness as the honeycomb, my bride;
>   milk and honey are under your tongue.
>   The fragrance of your garments is like that of
>   Lebanon.
> You are a garden locked up, my sister, my bride;
>   you are a spring enclosed, a sealed fountain.
> Your plants are an orchard of pomegranates
>   with choice fruits,
>   with henna and nard,
>   nard and saffron,
>   calamus and cinnamon,
>   with every kind of incense tree,
>   with myrrh and aloes
>   and all the finest spices. (Song of Songs 4:10–14)

There are at least ten fragrances identified in the Song, with additional references to fruits and other unidentified scents. We describe some of them below:

Nard (1:12)—Grown in the foothills of the Himalayas, nard has intense, warm, fragrant, musky notes.

Myrrh (1:13)—Derived from trees grown along the Red Sea, Abyssinia and India. The aroma is warm, fragrant, aromatic and slightly pungent.

Frankincense (3:6)—Extracted from trees grown in India, Arabia and the northeast coast of Africa. A warm, slightly citrine perfume, balsamic par excellence, still used in modern perfumery for its oriental notes.

Saffron (4:14)—Type of crocus that has purple flowers and produces an oil that gives a sweet, spicy, floral scent. The flower is native to western Asia, Asia Minor and the eastern Mediterranean. A single ounce of spice requires more than 4,000 individual blossoms.

Calamus (4:14)—From sweet cane oil, which has a warm, woody, spicy fragrance.

Cinnamon (4:14)—Produced from the aromatic bark of trees native to India, Ceylon and the far East. This well-known fragrance was considered in ancient times to be one of the most exquisite of fragrances.

Spices/Balsam (4:10)—The spice used in the anointing oil associated with the tabernacle (Exodus 25:6), and was one of the gifts brought to Solomon by the Queen of Sheba (1 Kings 10: 2, 10, 25). It is also

used in the beautification process undergone by
Esther (Esther 2:12).[3]

These are only a few of the oils and scents used by
the two lovers in the Song. It is fascinating to note that
the fragrances are usually mentioned in lists, and in the
same encounter. A plethora of scents cascaded from
their bodies, all to delight, titillate, enrapture, inspire
and excite their lover. As we read the Song we can feel
their passion—it is if they are asking themselves: "What
fragrances will there be, and where will I find them?"

As in our day, perfumes in ancient times were exot-
ic, rare and often quite costly. The delicate but expensive fragrances symbolize something very profound:
our love life is precious and worthy of our best effort
and costly investment. Money spent on our private love
is not a waste or a luxury. No, it is an investment in a
treasure given to us by God, a prize worth protecting
and nurturing. It is money invested in our most enduring and valued human relationship.[4] It is money spent

---

3. For more information on the fragrances mentioned here see Longman,
Song of Songs, 156–157; Carr, *The Song of Solomon,* 125–126, and Joseph C.
Dillow, *Solomon on Sex* (Nashville: Thomas Nelson, 1977), 83. Also see *The
Interpreter's Dictionary of the Bible, Vol. 3* (Nashville: Abington Press, 1962),
730–732.

4. The Gospel accounts of the women who anointed Jesus with precious
ointment (Matthew 26:6–13, Mark 14:1–9, Luke 7:36–50, John 12:1–8) certainly have relevance here. While their actions were completely spiritual in
nature, the principle of costly expression of our love is of enduring and uni-
versal application. What some criticized as "waste" (Mark 14:4) Jesus said
was "beautiful" (Matthew 26:10).

to keep our passion strong and our romantic fires burning brightly. Some of us can afford more than others, but let us all have an attitude of generosity when it comes to our marriages.

Now, how are you feeling about the kind of emphasis, thought and imagination that you need to put into your romantic life? Are you beginning to grasp the larger picture? A satisfying romantic life in marriage is not an automatic—it takes deliberate investment of ourselves and our resources. Far from being "impractical" or a waste, romance is worth your time, money and planning. If we rarely think about it, or relegate our love lives to a lesser place in our married life, our romance will suffer, along with our marriage. But the good news is that we reap what we sow—and if we sow generously in our love life, we will reap a rich reward.

The Location of Fragrance

Fragrance was in the room and in the air all around them. Lovemaking is all about atmosphere, and fragrance is a key element in setting the right mood. How is the ambience in your bedroom? Been lighting any scented candles lately? How about the bed itself—the sheets, the pillows, the bedspread—are they clean and fresh?

Your lips drop sweetness as the honeycomb, my bride;
    milk and honey are under your tongue.
The fragrance of your garments is like that of Lebanon.
(Song of Songs 4:11)

This lady's wardrobe (probably her intimate attire) was perfumed, and it caught her man's attention. Use perfume and cologne on your clothing, especially as you prepare for love. The scents will create an intoxicating and alluring world in which your sexual life will flourish.

Come away, my lover,
    and be like a gazelle
or like a young stag
    on the spice-laden mountains. (Song of Songs 8:14)

How much fragrance do we use? These lovers were generous, even lavish with their fragrances. Her perfume spread its aroma at the dinner table (1:12). He was like a column of smoke, perfumed with myrrh and incense (3:6). He said she was like a "mountain of myrrh" (4:6) and that her lips dripped sweetness (4:11). She commented that his lips were "like lilies dripping with myrrh" (5:13).

Certainly the amount of fragrance, and its intensity, are matters for each couple to decide. But, it is my guess that most of us err on the side of employing too little. In private, try being more generous, and see what happens. If we get more aroused and have a more satisfying sexual experience, then it's time for a permanent increase.[5]

Their breath was pleasant. His lips bore the fragrance of myrrh (5:13) her breath had the scent of apples (7:8). When we kiss our lover, we need to be encouraged, even intoxicated, by the sweet and refreshing air we breathe. That is all the more reason that we take care to make ourselves as inviting and pleasant as we can to our lover.

Where on our bodies do we use fragrance? Perhaps the question should be, "Where and how does it best promote attraction and affection?" The bride in the Song used fragrance in her most intimate sexual areas:

> Awake, north wind,
>   and come, south wind!
> Blow on my garden,
>   that its fragrance may spread abroad.
> Let my lover come into his garden
>   and taste its choice fruits. (Songs of Songs 4:16)

We will reserve the full exposition of this amazing

---

5. Some of us may have allergies that hinder the use of fragrance. I encourage couples not to readily or quickly surrender to this vexing malady, but to make a diligent search for those products that will work for both partners. But certainly if either partner does not prefer the use of fragrances, then it is not best for you.

passage for the chapter on taste, but let us observe that the fragrant "garden" to which she invited her lover was a euphemism for the most private and personal part of her anatomy. She calls upon her lover to taste and enjoy her, and says that she has prepared the area for his arrival with the most precious of oils and scents.

He responds in the next verse that he accepted her invitation, and that he took in her most intimate, feminine gift with all of its exciting and rhapsodic fragrance:

> I have come into my garden, my sister, my bride;
>> I have gathered my myrrh with my spice.
> I have eaten my honeycomb and my honey;
>> I have drunk my wine and my milk.
> (Song of Songs 5:1)

Let us remember that fragrance is a special gift from God. Married couples, may we imitate the lovers in the Song, not only in the use of fragrance, but in the sentiments of consideration and respect for each other that it reflects.

May we as husbands say of our wives:

> How delightful is your love, my sister, my bride!

How much more pleasing is your love than wine,
and the fragrance of your perfume than any spice!
(Song of Songs 4:10)

And may wives say of their husbands:

Pleasing is the fragrance of your perfumes;
your name is like perfume poured out.
No wonder the maidens love you!
(Song of Songs 1:3)

Chapter 5

The Tastes of Love

Your lips drop sweetness as the honeycomb, my bride;
  milk and honey are under your tongue.

Song of Songs 4:11

Awake, north wind,
  and come, south wind!
Blow on my garden,
  that its fragrance may spread abroad.
Let my lover come into his garden
  and taste its choice fruits.

Song of Songs 4:16

May...your mouth [be] like the best wine.
May the wine go straight to my lover,
  flowing gently over lips and teeth.

Song of Songs 7:8–9

If making love can be likened to a temple, we have now come to the holy of holies. Taste is the most intimate of all the senses. It is the most personal, the most private, the most exclusive of all the sensations we possess.

Think about it. To taste, you must open your mouth

and touch something to your tongue. You must take something inside your body, inside yourself, to taste it. Taste is completely voluntary, but not so the other senses; they are more readily accessible and more easily shared by, and with, other people. You can choose to make them intimate, but they are not necessarily so. But the sensation of taste is in a category all its own. It is always intimate, always personal, and always preceded by a decision—a decision of permission. Taste is the one sensation reserved for your spouse, and your spouse alone.[1]

It follows, then, that taste must be a special gift in lovemaking. It is the one sense we share exclusively with our lover. It is the most intimate sensation we give to one another. Who else is going to taste your body, except the one with whom you are one flesh?

If it is a special gift, it must provide unique rewards. It must give us, and our lover, something that no one else ever shares, or can share. It promises to be powerful, incendiary, titillating, delightful, ecstatic, thrilling and intense.

Taste is, well...a matter of taste. It is an intensely personal thing. Some like chocolate; others vanilla; some, kiwi-strawberry-lemon-lime, with a hint of hazel-

---

1. The only exception that comes to my mind is the relationship between a mother and her nursing infant, another of the most uniquely close interpersonal connections possible. But this is a relationship limited in duration, and a one-sided tasting experience, at that!

nut. There is no right or wrong—only what you like—and no one else can decide for you what that is.

> Taste is intense.
> Taste is subtle.
> Taste is personal—totally personal.
> Tastes are infinitely varied.
> Tastes change over time.

What are some of the tastes and flavors mentioned in the Song? Let's take a look at a few of them (emphasis mine):

> Like an apple tree among the trees of the forest
>   is my lover among the young men.
> I delight to sit in his shade,
>   and *his fruit is sweet to my taste.*
> He has taken me to the banquet hall,
>   and his banner over me is love.
> Strengthen me with *raisins,*
>   refresh me with *apples,*
>   for I am faint with love. (Song of Songs 2:3–5)

> Your lips drop sweetness as the *honeycomb,* my bride;
>   *milk and honey* are under your tongue.
> The fragrance of your garments is like that of Lebanon.
> (Song of Songs 4:11)

I have come into my garden, my sister, my bride;
 I have gathered my myrrh with my spice.
I have eaten my *honeycomb* and my *honey;*
 I have drunk my *wine* and my *milk.*
(Song of Songs 5:1)

His mouth is *sweetness* itself;
 he is altogether lovely.
This is my lover, this my friend,
 O daughters of Jerusalem. (Song of Songs 5:16)

May your breasts be like the clusters of the vine,
 the fragrance of your breath like *apples,*
 and your mouth like the best *wine.*
May the *wine* go straight to my lover,
 flowing gently over lips and teeth.
(Song of Songs 7:8, 9)

I would lead you
 and bring you to my mother's house—
 she who has taught me.
I would give you *spiced wine* to drink,
 the nectar of my *pomegranates.*
(Song of Songs 8:2)

Here is a list of some of the flavors mentioned:
 Fruits: Specifically raisins, apples, pomegranates.
 Spices.
 Milk.

Wine: Specifically blended wine and spiced wine.
Sweetness: Honey, the honeycomb.

Clearly, the sensation of taste is an intrinsic part of lovemaking. As a married couple, are you sensory-deprived in this area?

The Intimacy of Taste

Let's further explore the ways that taste can enhance our intimacy. Exactly what did the lovers in the Song taste?

Of course they tasted the flavors of the foods associated with their romantic encounters. Some of these tastes were literally the foods they enjoyed as they dined together, sharing moments of romance that led to sexual union. Who says that the romantic dinner is not an aphrodisiac? A shared meal, a glass of wine, a scrumptious dessert—all of these produce an atmosphere of pleasure, relaxation and sensory stimulation that increases our sexual desires.

But their tasting went beyond a nice meal shared together.

The Glory of the Kiss

Kissing on the lips is a form of intimacy mentioned repeatedly with great delight by the lovers in the Song.

Of course, not all kissing is sexual. There are kisses of greeting, given on the cheek. We give kisses like this to our family and friends, and in some cultures, even to strangers.

But these lovers aren't talking about those kinds of kisses. They are talking about sexual kisses, passionate kisses, deep kisses, prolonged kisses, kisses that involved the tongue, and intimate tasting of one another.

Listen to the following:

Let him kiss me with the kisses of his mouth
    for your love is more delightful than wine.
(Song of Songs 1:2)

Your lips drop sweetness as the honeycomb, my bride;
    milk and honey are under your tongue.
The fragrance of your garments
    is like that of Lebanon. (Song of Songs 4:11)

His cheeks are like beds of spice
    yielding perfume.
His lips are like lilies
    dripping with myrrh. (Song of Songs 5:13)

His mouth is sweetness itself;
    he is altogether lovely.
This is my lover, this my friend,
    O daughters of Jerusalem. (Song of Songs 5:16)

I said, "I will climb the palm tree;
   I will take hold of its fruit."
May your breasts be like the clusters of the vine,
   the fragrance of your breath like apples,
   and your mouth like the best wine.
May the wine go straight to my lover,
   flowing gently over lips and teeth.
(Song of Songs 7:8–9)

Several things are evident:

- They both enjoyed kissing each other.
- They longed to kiss each other, and expressed it clearly.
- Their kisses were deep, passionate, intimate and prolonged.
- Their kisses involved exploring and tasting each other with the tongue.

If kissing has departed from your marriage, bring it back. Kissing is one of the great gifts of sexual love. It combines touch, taste, fragrance, sight (unless you close your eyes the whole time), sound (words and…other sounds, too).

But kissing especially involves the two most intimate of the senses—taste and touch.

Kissing is, or can be:

- a way to remain intimate and close throughout the day
- a beginning
- progressive—it can lead to greater intimacy, arousal and passion
- continuous—it can go on throughout a time of intimacy
- an end—a satisfying way to conclude a time of sexual intercourse or to say goodnight at the conclusion of the day

Some of you are ready to end the chapter right now. "This is good," you are thinking. "We need to start kissing again, and with the passion and intimacy that we used to enjoy."

Oh no, we are not done yet, not nearly done yet.

The lovers in the Song have more to say, and more to teach us about the sense of taste in sexual love.

Are you ready to go to the next level?

The Garden Is Open

Some scholars say that the climax (oops!) of the book is the following section. Read these verses carefully, and begin to grasp what the lovers are really talking about. They are speaking clearly, yet subtly, with reserve and yet with boldness, and with poetic language, about a vital but (for many of us) off-limits subject. We are simply going to have to get comfortable with what God, through the Scriptures, is telling us here about the freedom, adventure, fun and intimacy of the sexual experience in married love—the freedom that he not only condones, but blesses. For clarity, I will break the section up according to the sentences spoken by the different characters:

Lover [Husband]
   You are a garden locked up, my sister, my bride;
      you are a spring enclosed, a sealed fountain.
   Your plants are an orchard of pomegranates
      with choice fruits,
      with henna and nard,
      nard and saffron,
      calamus and cinnamon,
      with every kind of incense tree,
      with myrrh and aloes
      and all the finest spices.
   You are a garden fountain,
      a well of flowing water
      streaming down from Lebanon.
(Song of Songs 4:12–15)

Beloved [Wife]
   Awake, north wind,
      and come, south wind!
   Blow on my garden,

> that its fragrance may spread abroad.
> Let my lover come into his garden
>   and taste its choice fruits.
> (Song of Solomon 4:16)

Lover [Husband]
> I have come into my garden, my sister, my bride;
>   I have gathered my myrrh with my spice.
> I have eaten my honeycomb and my honey;
>   I have drunk my wine and my milk.
> (Song of Songs 5:1)

What is the "garden locked up" to which the husband refers in verse 12 of chapter 4? The scholars tell us that this term is an erotic reference, a euphemism for the most intimate sexual areas of a woman's body. The "garden" or "fountain" is a way of describing the woman's vulva or vagina.[2] Now, think about it: aren't God's ways and words better than what we have come up with? Don't the descriptions in the Song leave us with a sense of beauty, delicacy and restraint—and yet with a sense of desire, freedom and passion? God knows how to create beauty and pleasure, and he knows how to describe it. We seem to go too far one way or the other—we are overmodest and afraid to talk about our bodies, or our words are flippant or brazen. And certainly, when people abandon a godly perspec-

---

2. Carr, *Song of Solomon,* 55–60; Longman, *Song of Songs,* 152–156; Dillow, *Solomon on Sex,* 81–86.

tive, it seems they can only talk about the body with words that are vulgar, dirty and dishonoring.

Left to our own devices, we just don't know how to have a discussion about this. Some of us opt for the clinical option, and while there is indeed a place for the medical terms of the surgeon or the coroner, it is not in the bedroom! As we read the Song, we see that there is an alternative that avoids both the textbook jargon of the scientist and the crassness of the world. There is a manner of expression that is beautiful, yet to the point. There are words that are glorious, but have a proper restraint. There is a way to speak sexually that is exciting, but not selfish and vulgar. I think these lovers get us in the right place, with the right words.

That being said, let's get down to business.

The husband says that his wife's "garden," while attractive and fragrant, is at present closed to him. The wife responds, by saying, in essence, "The garden is open to you. Yes, it is my garden, but as my husband, it is *yours*. I give it to you. I open it to you. I want to share it with you. It is all yours. Come in. Enjoy it. *Taste it*."

What happens in the interlude is not specifically stated. We do have these words of the husband, quoted earlier:

I have come into my garden, my sister, my bride;

I have gathered my myrrh with my spice.
I have eaten my honeycomb and my honey;
    I have drunk my wine and my milk.
(Song of Songs 5:1)

He is saying: "You gave me the key to your garden. You unlocked what was your most intimate physical possession and invited me in. You invited me in with your full consent, and with your full desire, to explore, enjoy and taste your garden. I have done so, and it was wonderful."

The section closes with the words of their friends, who, in support of their marital intimacies and joys, say, "Eat, drink and imbibe deeply, O lovers." And it is significant to note that the word translated "imbibe deeply" means to "be intoxicated" or "be drunk."

The pure ecstasy of total sensory enjoyment of her most intimate areas was his. It led to intoxication, the only intoxication that God allows—the intoxication of love. And sexual intoxication is the one "high" that comes closest to satisfying our desires for other-worldly pleasure.

Back to the Garden

Later on in the book, the bride returns to this theme of the garden:

> My lover has gone down to his garden,
>   to the beds of spices,
> to browse in the gardens
>   and to gather lilies.
> I am my lover's and my lover is mine;
>   he browses among the lilies. (Song of Songs 6:2–3)

And where were the lilies? The following verses give us some guidance:

> Your graceful legs are like jewels,
>   the work of a craftsman's hands.
> Your navel is a rounded goblet
>   that never lacks blended wine.
> Your waist is a mound of wheat
>   encircled by lilies. (Song of Songs 7:1b–2)

The lilies were located in her abdominal area, the place he goes to "browse" (compare 2:16).

As was pointed out earlier, the lovers in the Song speak euphemistically. The words translated "navel" and "waist" are a specific reference to the woman's genitalia and private sexual areas.[3] The goblet of blended wine from which he drinks, whatever meaning we choose to give it, indicates intimacy of the most personal kind.

---

3. Carr, *Song of Solomon*, 157–158; Longman, *Song of Songs*, 194–195; Dillow, *Solomon on Sex*, 133–134.

A Feast of Sexual Love

We are told in the Scriptures that when we are married we become one flesh—that God in some divine way joins husband and wife together. "They are no longer two, but one," Jesus says (Matthew 19:6). We are told that our bodies belong to each other. We are told that we are to seek to please each other.

Can we not begin to see just what that means? Can we not begin to see that in marriage our bodies are sacred, and yet to be enjoyed—fully enjoyed—by one another?

It is my experience in counseling that most married couples, including Christian married couples, are not enjoying the fullness of sexual joy and excitement that is intended for them. The reason for this may be due to false modesty, or to some sort of overreaction to the sin we see in the illicit relationships around us.

Our kisses are to be enjoyed. We drink deeply of the sensual pleasure and stimulation of passionate and intense joining of our lips and tongues. We kiss and taste each other's bodies. We are free to give and to taste each other's bodies wherever we wish, wherever we both are pleased to do so. It is ours by God-given design and by God-given right.

It is time for married couples to claim their gifts. It is time for husbands and wives to shed the unbiblical shackles of a mechanistic, boring and routine sex life. It is time to cast aside false modesty and the false belief that sex, and the enjoyment of our spouse's body and their enjoyment of ours, is somehow tainted, twisted or perverted.

This is not an attempt to tell any married couple exactly what to do or how to go about having sex. The Song is not that either. What it does do, however, is give us a picture of what can be and of the freedom that is ours to enjoy.

Tastes change. When we were young, we liked some foods that we now don't enjoy as much or that we no longer like at all. Foods that we once did not enjoy have now become our favorites. As we mature, we acquire new tastes over time.

The sexual practices in marriage are somewhat like that. At first, our tastes are simple. We are quite pleased with a basic menu. Later, however, we find that our tastes change and mature. We expand our horizons. We explore, we try new experiences. Activities we were not aware of or not ready for have now come in season. We find that there are more subtle and exquisite flavors to discover and enjoy.

If our sexual menu has stayed the same for many years, the Song says that there are more items for us to consider, and more options to enjoy than we before thought available. No, we don't have to do what other people do. And no, we don't have to do, nor should we do, anything which goes against our scruples or that is unpleasant to us or our partner. Love for one another forbids us from insisting on our own way. But, love for one another also means that we will consider another way, if it pleases the one we love.

You can work this out in the privacy of your own bedroom. But let these thoughts, and these words from the Song, help you to realize that God, in his goodness and love, has designed your body, and intends it to be lovingly given, tenderly enjoyed and joyfully pleasured by your partner. As far as our Creator is concerned, there are no off-limit areas. There is no wine, no fruit, no honey or honeycomb that is not meant to be tasted, enjoyed and shared with the one you love. We need only to claim it and enjoy it.

Has your love life become bland? Has your sex life lost its savor? Are you bored and unsatisfied? Maybe what you are missing is the taste of your partner—in all of its sweetness, spice and variety—all that your Creator lovingly plans for you to enjoy.

May we say, as was said in the Song: *My lover, the garden is open!*

Chapter 6

The Touch of Love

His left arm is under my head,
  and his right arm embraces me.
                    Song of Songs 2:6

My lover is mine and I am his;
  he browses among the lilies.
                    Song of Songs 2:16

Your stature is like that of the palm,
  and your breasts like clusters of fruit.
I said, "I will climb the palm tree;
  I will take hold of its fruit."
May your breasts be like the clusters of the vine,
  the fragrance of your breath like apples,
  and your mouth like the best wine.
May the wine go straight to my lover,
  flowing gently over lips and teeth.
                    Song of Songs 7:7–9

Intimacy of touch is the ultimate sensation of love-making. It is the deep pleasure of physical contact with our spouse that provides sexual arousal, stimulation and pleasure. It is this drive for excitement and ecstasy that gives our love life its intensity and its joy. We have saved touch for last because it is indeed the glory, goal and greatness of sexual love. The other four senses must ultimately be combined with touch for our sexual experience to be fulfilling. It is touch that engenders the beauty, fire and thrill of sexual love in marriage.

Touch is perhaps the most pervasive sense we possess. Our bodies are covered with nerve endings. They are given us by God to register pleasure and pain, hot and cold, rough and smooth, soft and hard, and myriad other sensations that defy description. For a husband and wife to experience the sexual joy that God intends, it will take a lifetime of discovery. They will spend years exploring the ways, through the mysterious and powerful sense of touch, that they can both arouse their partner's desire and bring them to a place of contentment and satisfaction.

Touch in the Song

The lovers in the Song share with us their rich indulgence in this wonderful sense.

He touches her hair, and is so attracted to it that he feels captivated by it.

> Your hair is like royal tapestry;
>   the king is held captive by its tresses.
> (Song of Songs 7:5b)

*He gently cradles her head in his left hand and holds her
with his right hand, caressing her and pulling her body
to his in a sensory feast of total body contact.*

> His left arm is under my head,
>> and his right arm embraces me. (Song of Songs 2:6)

He longs to caress her breasts.

He compares her body to a statuesque and graceful
palm tree, and her breasts to its fruit. He desires to
"climb" the tree, progressing his way up from her feet
to her head. He wants to caress and stroke her entire
body, bottom to top! And the reward of his ascent will
be the feel of her breasts and the kiss of her lips.

> Your stature is like that of the palm,
>> and your breasts like clusters of fruit.
> I said, "I will climb the palm tree;
>> I will take hold of its fruit."
> May your breasts be like the clusters of the vine,
>> the fragrance of your breath like apples,
>> and your mouth like the best wine.
> (Song of Songs 7:7–9)

This same sentiment is echoed in the Proverbs,
where the husband is told to always be "satisfied" by
his wife's breasts and "captivated" by her love:[1]

---

1. The Hebrew word here translated "satisfied" can also be rendered "to
be saturated, to drink one's fill."

May your fountain be blessed,
   and may you rejoice in the wife of your youth.
A loving doe, a graceful deer—
    may her breasts satisfy you always,
    may you ever be captivated by her love.
(Proverbs 5:18–19)

It might be difficult for some women to understand the sensual power and allure their breasts have for their husbands. While there are some men who are less drawn to this feature than to other attributes of their wife's anatomy, most husbands are indeed set on fire by their wife's endowment. While men and women both know that the breast has the practical purpose of nursing infant children, the male gender maintains that use is only *temporary*—the permanent and abiding function of their wife's breasts is in sexual attraction and pleasure. The loveliness of the feminine breast, with its power to arouse men, is designed by God himself. Most men believe the curvature, tenderness, coloration and shape of their wife's breasts to be one of the most glorious sights they have ever seen, and that to caress and kiss them is as close to an experience of pure delight as they will have in life.

Wives, do not dismiss, be mystified or be offended by your husband's desire to linger over this particular feature. It is one of your most glorious God-given assets. Appreciate and be flattered by your husband's attraction and attention. Let me say what I am about to say as politely as I can, and with appropriate dignity and reserve: women, your breasts are designed with a sexual response mechanism. Know with certainty that the reaction of your breasts to your husband's tactile attentions only serves to take you both to a higher place of arousal and joy in your lovemaking. Surrender yourself fully to your husband while helping him to understand your own changing and particular anatomical sensitivities in this area, and you will both be richly rewarded.

Both partners in the Song use oils as an enhancement to lovemaking.

> "Your oils have a pleasing fragrance,
>   Your name is like purified oil;
>   Therefore the maidens love you."
> (Song of Solomon 1:3, NASB)

> "How beautiful is your love, my sister, my bride!
>   How much better is your love than wine,
>   And the fragrance of your oils
>   Than all kinds of spices!"
> (Song of Solomon 4:10, NASB)

These precious liquids were not only fragrant, but pleasant to the touch. They augmented tactile sensation with their softening, sensual and lubricating powers.[2] Touching a highly sensitive area can be uncomfortable, even irritating, if the skin is not properly conditioned. For touch to be free and fully satisfying, some areas of the body will require moisturizing and lubrication. Smooth, sleek skin is an aphrodisiac. It allows, encourages and invites freedom of sexual touch. Try adding fragrant, silken oils to your love life and your sense of touch will come alive with pleasure.

The lovers in the Song rhapsodize about their kisses.
The bride craves her husband's kiss, claiming it is better even than wine:

> Let him kiss me with the kisses of his mouth—
>   for your love is more delightful than wine.
> (Song of Songs 1:2)

Likewise, the husband yearns for his wife's kiss:

> May...the fragrance of your breath [be] like apples,
>   and your mouth like the best wine.
> (Song of Songs 7:8–9)

---

2. "The aromatic anointing oils helped replace the natural skin oils lost to the heat and dryness of the climate; they were more than just perfumes." Carr, *The Song of Solomon,* 121–122.

And she responds by saying that she wants her kiss to flow sensually over his lips and teeth:

> May the wine go straight to my lover,
>   flowing gently over lips and teeth.
> (Song of Songs 7:9b)

He touched her intimately in his kisses, saying that he gathered the sweetness of her lips and the milk and honey that were under her tongue:

> Your lips drop sweetness as the honeycomb, my bride;
>   milk and honey are under your tongue.
> (Song of Songs 4:11)

These kisses are not just little pecks on the cheek, or brief expressions of courteous greeting—they are deep, passionate, prolonged, sensual and stimulating. The lovers fully touched each others' lips, tongues, and palates. All the sensitive nerves were awakened and brought to their full sensory arousal.

The lovers touched, caressed and fondled one another's bodies.

> My lover has gone down to his garden,
>   to the beds of spices,
> to browse in the gardens

and to gather lilies.
I am my lover's and my lover is mine;
     he browses among the lilies. (Song of Songs 6:2–3)

It is only logical that all of the touching that occurs between them should lead to touching, kissing and otherwise stimulating the most intensely sensitive sexual areas of the body. He touches, and she enjoys. And of course, the touching was most certainly mutual, as she, like he, touched and tasted him intimately:

Like an apple tree among the trees of the forest
     is my lover among the young men.
I delight to sit in his shade,
     and his fruit is sweet to my taste.
(Song of Songs 2:3)

Getting in Touch with Touch

So what have we learned?

Touch is pervasive.

Nerve endings cover literally every square inch of our skin. They are put there by God for good reason. Some areas of our bodies and their accompanying sensations seem to have nothing to do with sex, but...think again. The sexual power of touch is not limited to the commonly thought of erotic areas of the body. Sexual stimulation, oddly enough, can only come when we initially relax and become comfortable. Some nerves need to be stimulated to achieve sexual pleasure, but others need the opposite—they need to be relaxed in order for us to have a sexual experience. This is one of the ironies that reveal God's sense of humor! Satisfying sex cannot occur while negative sensations or emotions are coursing through our bodies, or when our nerves, muscles and bodies are racked with anxiety and tension.

Touch is progressive.

If we want to have a sex life that is powered by touch, we will need to start touching each other! That observation may sound obvious, yet many of us forget to express physical affection throughout the day.

Sexual touch is best aroused by a slow progression. Men tend to want to go straight to the most intense area. But for women, the other five senses are especially key in preparing for intimate touch—as is emotional closeness throughout the day. Touch each other in nonsexual areas. Hold hands. Sit close to each other. Give a kiss of greeting and goodbye. Give a little shoulder massage or caress of the arm as you walk by your spouse. Stroke her hair as you speak to her. Gently touch his cheek or his elbow as you converse over a cup of coffee, or share a brief moment together.

Do these things, and watch what happens—no, *feel* what happens. In expressing physical affection you create an atmosphere, a universe of touch in your marriage. You break through the loneliness, the isolation, the barrenness of contact that you experience in daily life. You awaken your body, you awaken your nerves, you awaken your feelings...you long for more. And, you are prepared for more when the opportunity comes. You aren't jumping from dead zero to lightspeed, you are just accelerating what has already begun to move.

If there is one thing many women would like to say to their husbands about touch, it is this:

> *Don't touch me just when you are in the mood for sex. Touch me to show me you love me, care for me, and think about me throughout the day. Show me that your touch is not just a prelude to satisfying your own desires, but a longing to unite with me and enjoy our relationship. Please touch me, but touch me as a part of our whole life together. Then, I will be able to give myself to you and enjoy the thrill of intimate touch with you as never before.*

Perhaps one way to show the progress of touch is this:

The touch of attention
The touch of affection
The touch of attraction
The touch of arousal
The touch of pleasure
The touch of ecstasy
The touch of satisfaction

This is not to say that a husband and wife have to go through a long stage of preparation for every sexual encounter. No, the "quickie" has its essential place of joy and pleasure in the sexual repertoire of a happily married couple. But you will find that couples who can easily and spontaneously have a quick sexual encounter are couples who are close, and who are comfortable touching each other throughout the day. The quick surrender, the stolen moment, comes easy to them because they keep the fires of ardor burning by being physically and emotionally connected throughout the day.

What areas are we to touch? After reading the Song, we might better ask, "What areas are we not to touch?" Let's think about it this way:

God is our creator.

God created the human body.

God created the human body with the capacity for the enjoyment of the sense of touch, including sexual touch.

God created numerous areas of the human body that respond to sexual stimulation.

God created specific areas with concentrated amounts and types of nerves that respond intensively to sexual stimulation, bringing both men and women to sexual climax.

In summary, God gave us our nerve endings for a good reason. *If the body has nerves that respond to stimulation, then they were purposefully and lovingly designed that way.* Function follows form. This means that in marriage we are completely free to enjoy receiving and giving pleasure wherever and however we wish.

Do we think that God makes us with the nerve endings that cry out for and respond to stimulation and arousal, but then says, "Hold it! That's off limits; no trespassing there!"? In marriage, as far as the divine plan is concerned, there is no place on your body, or on your spouse's body, that is untouchable. Within the bounds of your own personal wishes, you have the freedom, without any biblical limitation of conscience, to fully enjoy your partner's body. There is no part of our bodies that is evil, dirty, unclean or ugly. God made it all, and it is all good—very good.

Making the Application

Where does this knowledge leave us, or better yet, where does it take us?

Many of us have been far too limited in our enjoyment of the sense of touch in our love lives. Sex, for too many couples, is no more than functional, rudimentary intercourse. Our sexual experience consists of vaginal penetration and male release—accomplished as quickly as possible. How far this is from the romantic and exciting lovemaking of the husband and wife in the Song, and how far it is from the joy of sexual pleasure intended for us by God! No wonder many people are frustrated in their marriages and have given up the hope of having a fiery and fulfilling sex life with their spouse.

If you have previously thought that God's plan for lovemaking in marriage is emotionless, mechanical intercourse, you have been mistaken. It is my happy duty to say that the truth is otherwise—and the truth will set you free! A new world of sensation awaits you.

Let's loosen up, drop our uptight ideas, and begin to enjoy our freedom. Let's liberate our consciences from our unbiblical shackles. Let's get rid of our fears, guilt and embarrassment. Let us enjoy exploring and being explored, touching and being touched, caressing and being caressed. When God made Adam and Eve, they were unclothed, free and unashamed. They possessed each other in purity and in innocence.

In marriage—*your* marriage—God has decreed that your bodies belong to each other. Yes, we may need some time and some experience to begin to enjoy each other as fully as we are allowed. Yes, we may need to grow in closeness to each other, patiently allowing some practices to come to us by delicious discovery over the months and years. This is a part of the reward of being married for a lifetime. But never let it be said of us that we, through some sort of misguided prudishness or false understanding of holiness, hold back from the full, exciting and enthusiastic sexual joy that God intends for every married couple to know.

Chapter 7

My Sister, My Bride: Wife

You have stolen my heart, my sister, my bride;
   you have stolen my heart
with one glance of your eyes,
   with one jewel of your necklace.
How delightful is your love, my sister, my bride!
   How much more pleasing is your love than wine,
   and the fragrance of your perfume than any spice!

                        Song of Songs 4:9–10

So, beloved sisters and brides, how are you feeling? Are you having fun yet?

I wonder if some of the women reading this book are a little overwhelmed right now:

> *"If this is the standard, I'm sunk. I'm no sex kitten—never have been, never will be. I have kids. I have a job. I have extra pounds. I'm just not as motivated as I ought to be. I feel inadequate and incapable."*

Some of you may be a little peeved:

*"Thanks a lot, Sam. You have now set my hus-
band's standards so high that I will never be able
to make him happy. Get real! Life is not one long
honeymoon, buster!"*

Others may be skeptical:

*"Just who is that woman in the story anyway?
She sounds oversexed to me. No married woman
in her right mind can be like that."*

Okay, everybody, take a deep breath—several of
them—and let's take a look at what kind of expectations we need to have of ourselves.

Marriage: Seeing the Big Picture

Let's go back to the beginning—the literal beginning, in Genesis—when God laid out the master plan.

Men and women were created with a common purpose—to serve and glorify God. God has a purpose for
your life that includes, but extends far beyond, your
relationship with your husband and children. Let's
understand that from the get-go.

And let's realize that people don't have to be married in order to fulfill God's purpose in their life. But the
Scriptures tell us that, for most people, marriage is both
needed and best, and in that relationship, both partners

have a role to play. We especially want to learn God's plan for wives, and what role he intended for sex to play in marriage.

But let's take a different approach. Rather than begin by examining how God made women, let's take a look at how he made *men*. Why start here? It is because when women understand the needs God placed in men, then they can get a handle on what God expects of them in marriage.

After he created man, God saw that he was lonely and incomplete without woman. (The thunderous *Amen!* you just heard comes from the united voices of all husbands in the world!) God decided to do something about this situation, and life for men took a radical turn for the better:

> The LORD God said, "It is not good for the man to be alone. I will make a helper suitable for him." (Genesis 2:18)

Since the male gender was incomplete without the female counterpart, God made women to be their completer, complement and partner—the ones who supply what was divinely left out in men. Rather than look at this as insinuating that women are inferior to men (a completely unbiblical concept) look at it this way: women were the essential missing element, the crowning glory, the last, spectacular exercise of God's power in the awe-inspiring drama of creation.

One of your great purposes in marriage, then, is to please God by being the best completer of your husband that you can be. While many of his needs are the same as yours, he has others that are radically different. The more you come to understand these differences and meet these needs, the better your marriage will be. You can be certain that your womanly qualities—along with your own personal characteristics—are desperately needed by your husband. Yes, he needs you, and he needs you deeply. God says so, and in their heart of hearts, men know it, too.

But where does that leave you, and where does that leave women as a whole? Are you just here to please your husband, with no real value of your own? Of course not. The truth that follows is of vital importance: *seeking to lovingly meet your husband's needs is the pathway to your own happiness and fulfillment in your marriage.* Paradoxically, when we lose ourselves, we find ourselves (Luke 9:24). This complex reality holds true not only in marriage, but in life and relationships in general.

Trust this. Better yet, trust *God.*

Does this help? Does it make sense? Your roles are as follows:

Companion: His best friend, the person with whom he spends the rest of his life. You never leave him, and he never leaves you.

Complement: You balance him; you supply strengths he does not possess. Together each of you is a better person than you are alone. Together you make a better picture of Jesus than either of you does by yourself. You make him whole. You supply what is missing. Your presence in his life makes him a better man.

Cooperation: You work with him, not against him, and not independent of him. You combine forces, you work together. United, you get more done, and do it better and easier. Together you do what you could not do alone.

Pretty exciting when we see it this way, isn't it? Now that we see the big picture, I'll bet you know what's coming next.

How Romance Fits In

The sexual relationship is a vital element of the partnership of marriage. And this is where the Song of Songs comes in.

Divine wisdom has given you the bride in this story

as a mentor. She is not just some crazy, wild woman to make you blush as you read of her passionate marriage—she is the ideal God puts before you! She is to serve as your example, your leader, your trailblazer. As such, she is worthy of trust, respect and imitation.

We don't know what she looked like. We don't know how tall she was, how she carried herself, how her voice sounded. We don't know where she shopped, or what cosmetics she used. We don't even know precisely what she did in bed to please and excite her husband. What we do know is that she had some romantic attitudes and actions that are endorsed by God. As a wife, you can look at her and learn, with the confidence that you are on the road that leads to sexual joy and fulfillment for both you and your husband.

Romantic Characteristics

Let's take another look at her and get some inside information on romantic relations—better than any advice you will ever get from a woman's magazine or talk show. We are going to look at seven attributes and attitudes. Learn them, employ them, and watch your husband come to life and your marriage reclaim its fire.

1. She Is Sexually Alive, Aware and Animated

Like an apple tree among the trees of the forest

is my lover among the young men.
I delight to sit in his shade,
   and his fruit is sweet to my taste.
He has taken me to the banquet hall,
   and his banner over me is love.
Strengthen me with raisins,
   refresh me with apples,
   for I am faint with love. (Song of Songs 2:3–5)

This lady enjoys sex! She delights in it. She loves it so much she is either fainting with anticipation as she contemplates union with her husband or she is so worn out from lovemaking that she must replenish her energy.

What do you say, wives? Can you let her example take you higher? Are you ready to grow as a sexual woman? We strive to grow in other areas; what about here? What is there to lose? There is absolutely nothing dirty, unladylike or vulgar about being fired up about sex. It is right, good and godly to be thrilled about making love with your husband. What I am about to recommend won't and can't happen every night, but...hang on, here we go...

Let yourself go, drop your guard, and have some fun. Let out the seductive tigress your husband thought he married and would love to have to tame. Break out of your mold. You may be quiet, modest and demure most of the time, but that doesn't have to be who you are in the bedroom. You may be a lady of reserved, controlled elegance, but your husband would be happy for you to show him your wild side. Perhaps your sex drive lies dormant, or has atrophied or diminished, but it can awaken and come alive. Maybe childbearing, illness or age has taken a toll. Perhaps your husband seems disinterested. Don't be discouraged. Believe that God will help you, and your man, to rekindle the embers to a blazing flame.

2. She Is Sexually At Ease

> O daughters of Jerusalem, I charge you—
>   if you find my lover,
> what will you tell him?
>   Tell him I am faint with love. (Song of Songs 5:8)

Here is a woman who is comfortable with her sexuality. She talks about it with ease. She talks to her girlfriends about her man and her feelings. She talks to her husband about her needs, desires and intentions with candor, openness and zest. As a matter of fact, she does most of the talking about sex in the Song—much more than her husband does. And while she is never coarse, vulgar or unfeminine in her manner, she feels at home with her sexual drive, her sexual power and her sexual self.

3. She Is Sexually Assured

Talk about confidence—this lady has it in spades! She is confident that her husband finds her desirable:

> I belong to my lover,
>   and his desire is for me. (Song of Songs 7:10)

She is confident that she can please him:

> Let us go early to the vineyards
>   to see if the vines have budded,
> if their blossoms have opened,
>   and if the pomegranates are in bloom—
>   there I will give you my love.
> The mandrakes send out their fragrance,
>   and at our door is every delicacy,
> both new and old,
>   that I have stored up for you, my lover.
> (Song of Songs 7:12–13)

She is confident she is attractive:

> Dark am I, yet lovely,
>   O daughters of Jerusalem.... (Song of Songs 1:5)

> I am a rose of Sharon,
>   a lily of the valleys. (Song of Songs 2:1)

Here is how it works: the more confident you are about yourself, the more radiant and beautiful you become. Certainly you should do the best you can to dress becomingly and keep yourself attractive, but be happy with who you are. Don't fall into the trap of running yourself down or comparing yourself unfavorably to other women. Remember that you are made in the image of God, that it was he who formed you in your mother's womb (Psalm 139), and he likes you just the way he made you. Furthermore, your husband didn't make a mistake when he married you—he was the smartest guy in town! Your looks attracted him when he first met you, and they can light him up again.

4. She Is Arousing and Able to Be Aroused

I have taken off my robe—
   must I put it on again?
I have washed my feet—
   must I soil them again?
My lover thrust his hand through the latch-opening;
my heart began to pound for him.
   I arose to open for my lover,
and my hands dripped with myrrh,
   my fingers with flowing myrrh,
on the handles of the lock. (Song of Songs 5:3–5)

Allow yourself to be aroused. Let your husband take

you to some realms of delight you have never seen before. Enjoy the bodily sensations that God has given you. Don't let an over-analytical mind get in the way of your instincts. Relax, enjoy yourself and your husband, and you will probably find there is more passion in you than you ever knew. Even if your arousal is more emotional than physical, enjoy it. And, however you may be feeling, learn to enjoy getting him excited.

Some wives are their own worst enemy here. They psych themselves out: "Oh no, I'm not aroused. I'm not responding—something's wrong with me!" If you think like this, you are getting in your own way. Instead, let your motto be the one that the beloved bride repeats to her female friends:

> Daughters of Jerusalem, I charge you
>   by the gazelles and by the does of the field:
> Do not arouse or awaken love
>   until it so desires.
> (Song of Songs 2:7, compare 3:5, 8:4)

Stop worrying about your sex drive and let it come as it will. When you make love, let whatever happens, happen. Your man is wired differently than you—he usually has to have an orgasm to have a satisfying encounter. With you, it might be more about love and closeness. That, too, is arousal!

5. She Is Assertive

She takes the initiative. She is feminine and digni-fied, but she is quite aggressive in initiating sex:

Let him kiss me with the kisses of his mouth—
    for your love is more delightful than wine.
(Song of Songs 1:2)

Take me away with you—let us hurry!
    Let the king bring me into his chambers.
(Song of Songs 1:4)

If you really want to give your husband a thrill, if you want to capture his attention and rivet his thoughts on you, invite him to make love. Let him know you are ready, willing and available. Some of you may be think-ing, "That sounds good, but my husband is not interest-ed in me." Okay, maybe things haven't been where they need to be, but don't let that defeat you. Be assertive, take some risks. Light the candles and break out that sexy lingerie. As men say about sports, "You miss every shot you don't take." Be willing to keep shooting until you hit the target!

6. She Is Adventurous

Most men are turned on by sex that is adventurous and edgy. I am not talking about perversion, pornography or pain. I am talking about romantic relations that are spontaneous, imaginative, fun and playful. Enjoy learning some new ways to tease and please each other. Try making love in some new places and in some different positions. Break out of the boredom; get out of your rut. Unleash your creative side.

Our heroine makes some exciting suggestions and does some exciting things:

Outdoor love:

> Our bed is lush with foliage;
>   the beams of our house are cedars,
>   and our rafters are cypresses.
> (Song of Songs 1:16–17, Christian Standard Bible)

You can check it out for yourself, but most scholars agree, this verse means they enjoyed making love *alfresco*, or in the open air!

Sex in the country:

> Come, my love, let's go to the field;
>   let's spend the night among the henna blossoms.
> Let's go early to the vineyards;
>   let's see if the vine has budded,
> if the blossom has opened,

> if the pomegranates are in bloom.
> There I will give you my love.
> (Song of Songs 7:11–12, Christian Standard Bible)

Let's try my mother's house:

> I would lead you,
>> I would take you, to the house of my mother who
>> taught me.
> I would give you spiced wine to drink from my pome-
>> granate juice.
> His left hand is under my head,
>> and his right hand embraces me.
> (Song of Songs 8:2–3, Christian Standard Bible)

Shall I dance?

> *Friends*
> Come back, come back, O Shulammite;
>> come back, come back, that we may gaze on you!

> *Lover [the husband]*
> Why would you gaze on the Shulammite
>> as on the dance of Mahanaim?
> (Song of Songs 6:13)

As she dances, he begins to compliment her appearance (7:1ff). He starts with her sandaled feet, and works his way up her body, describing it in poetic, sensual detail.[1] What did she have on? What *didn't* she have on? By the end of his visual journey up her swaying body, he is ready for more than just watching:

> How beautiful you are and how pleasing,
>> O love, with your delights!
> Your stature is like that of the palm,
>> and your breasts like clusters of fruit.
> I said, "I will climb the palm tree;
>> I will take hold of its fruit."
> May your breasts be like the clusters of the vine,
>> the fragrance of your breath like apples,
>> and your mouth like the best wine.
> (Song of Songs 7:6–9)

Dancing with your husband and for your husband may just be the adventure that he is looking for, and that your love life needs. Why not give it a try? You say you aren't a good dancer? *It is a God-given instinct.* Embarrassed? *Sister, you are the only performer; you are the star of the show.* There is only one judge in this

---

1. This is an admittedly difficult passage to interpret. Is she a part of a public dance and being observed by the "friends?" Is she privately dancing for, or with, her husband? Is she dancing at all? The strongest argument for her actually dancing is found in the verses that follow. Commentators offer that it is her sandaled feet, moving in dance, that first catch her husband's eye. His strongly sensual description of her that immediately follows 6:13 is certainly more appropriate for a private occasion than a public one. For a strong presentation of this view see Dillow, *Solomon on Sex,* 131–147. Also see Longman, *Song of Songs,* 188–194, and Carr, *The Song of Solomon,* 155–156. The overall interpretation of the Song is in my view best served when we assume an understated, but powerful sexual content rather than a tamer version.

contest, and he will be so excited by what he sees that he will be ready to come over and tear your clothes off, if they aren't already off.

So, beloved sisters, stop being tentative and conservative. Have some fun. Tease him. Play a little. Get out on the edge. Take a risk, surprise him. Hit him with all five senses!

7. She Is Admiring

My lover is radiant and ruddy,
    outstanding among ten thousand.
His head is purest gold;
    his hair is wavy
    and black as a raven.
His eyes are like doves
    by the water streams,
washed in milk,
    mounted like jewels.
His cheeks are like beds of spice
    yielding perfume.
His lips are like lilies
    dripping with myrrh.
His arms are rods of gold
    set with chrysolite.
His body is like polished ivory
    decorated with sapphires.
His legs are pillars of marble
    set on bases of pure gold.

His appearance is like Lebanon,
　　choice as its cedars.
His mouth is sweetness itself;
　　he is altogether lovely.
This is my lover, this my friend,
　　O daughters of Jerusalem. (Song of Songs 9:10–16)

No man can perform sexually if he feels unappreciated and disrespected. Expressing ridicule, or even being insensitive in what you say about his appearance or lovemaking is de-motivating to him. If you are picking at your husband and finding negative things to say, then you are pouring cold water on the fire of your romantic life. He will fight back, or he will withdraw and harden his heart. Don't let it happen! Build him up. Tell him when he looks great and smells great. Commend him on his skill as a lover. He will live up to your praise, but it is hard for him to overcome your criticisms.

Most women do not understand how much men need them to notice and compliment their appearance. The need may not be as salient in men as it is in women, but it is there nonetheless. Men respond with excitement when their wives notice them and make encouraging remarks about the way they look. Try it, wives. Give your husband some specific positive comments about his physique and appearance, and watch what happens. He will stand a little taller, laugh a little louder, and will in all likelihood want to snuggle up a little closer. It will make him more confident and gentle, and round off some of his rough edges. It might also motivate him to stay in shape, take better care of himself, and dress with more awareness. And you will reap the reward of having a warmer, more sensitive and motivated lover.

Sometimes compliments can backfire, though. My brilliant, multitalented wife possesses a rare gift for creating malapropisms, and has delightful way of switching words around. As Geri and I have grown older, we have had to face the sexual challenges that come with the territory. After one romantic evening together, we were lying side by side, dreamily basking in the moment. Geri, wanting to commend me on my masculine prowess and virility, turned to me and said, "Well for an older man, you sure are *viral!*"

One Who Brings Contentment

As the Song comes to a close, we find a fascinating verse, one that I hope will inspire the wives who read this book:

Thus I have become in his eyes
   like one bringing contentment.
(Song of Songs 8:10b)

The Hebrew word *shalom*, here translated "contentment" is still used in greetings by Jewish people today. It can also be translated "peace," but its meaning is greater than our translations reveal. *Shalom* is not just the absence of strife, but the presence of fulfillment, satisfaction, peace, contentment and wholeness. With this greeting you are being wished the fullness of God's care, blessing, abundance and well-being that warms you to the core.

As the book closes and the bride reflects on her relationship with her husband, she expresses her heart—she is the one who brings to her husband the gift of *shalom.*

Wives, may you grow in your God-given role, and may you succeed in your glorious and divine mission: to fulfill your husband's deepest needs—in body, soul, mind and heart.

Shalom!

Chapter 8

My Friend, My Lover: Husband

My lover is radiant and ruddy,
  outstanding among ten thousand.
                              Song of Songs 5:10

Like an apple tree among the trees of the forest
  is my lover among the young men.
I delight to sit in his shade,
  and his fruit is sweet to my taste.
                              Song of Songs 2:3

Okay, husbands, your turn. We have looked at the general lessons that apply to both partners. What can we learn from the Song about how we *as men* need to think and behave in order to have a great sex life with our wives? We will address four areas.

1. Commitment, Companionship and Closeness

Men, I am about to tell you the most important fact you will ever learn about how your wife thinks about sex. If you get anything out of this book, get this! Blessed is the man who understands, accepts and lives in harmony with his wife's God-given sexuality.

Here it is, Love Lesson #1:

For her, sex is about your *total relationship.*

Her sexual union with you is based upon, nurtured and inspired by *commitment, companionship and closeness.* The only way she can fully respond to you sexually is if she believes and knows in her heart that the two of you have a sacred and secure relationship of love. For your wife to be excited and motivated sexually, she must feel close to you and be confident that you deeply and dearly love her.

Sex proceeds out of this commitment, not the other way around. And guess what? God has designed it this way. The need for closeness *before* sex is not a feminine foible or weakness. It is a divinely given gift, a gift that you as a husband must understand and respect, and with which you must work in harmony.

Women want to know that they are the one and only woman in your life—for all of your life. Listen to this request made by the bride in the Song:

> Place me like a seal over your heart,
>   like a seal on your arm;
> for love is as strong as death,
>   its jealousy unyielding as the grave.
> It burns like blazing fire,

like a mighty flame.
Many waters cannot quench love;
    rivers cannot wash it away.
If one were to give
    all the wealth of his house for love,
    it would be utterly scorned. (Song of Songs 8:6–7)

So how do we assure and reassure our wife that she has our full commitment? One of the most powerful ways is with our *words*. The husband in the Song excels in assuring his wife of her unique place in his life.

He lets her know that she owns his heart:

You have stolen my heart, my sister, my bride;
    you have stolen my heart
with one glance of your eyes,
    with one jewel of your necklace. (Song of Songs 4:9)

He lets her know that, though there may be other beautiful women, she is unique, one-of a-kind. He assures her that there is no one else like her in his life, that she has no competition for his affections, desires and love:

Sixty queens there may be,
    and eighty concubines,
    and virgins beyond number;
but my dove, my perfect one, is unique.
(Song of Songs 6:8–9)

He warms her heart with his endearing names: six times he calls her his "bride."[1] What does that say to her? It says he still regards her as the beautiful bride with whom he fell in love and to whom he made a marriage vow, and pledged life-long fidelity.

Nine times he calls her his "darling."[2] This Hebrew word also has in its meaning the concept of "companion." In other words, he recognizes that his wife is not just there to meet his sexual needs—she is to be his best friend, lifelong partner and closest confidant.

But he does more than talk. He takes action. He invites her to go away alone together:

"Arise, my darling,
     my beautiful one, and come with me.
See! The winter is past;
     the rains are over and gone.
Flowers appear on the earth;
     the season of singing has come,
the cooing of doves
     is heard in our land.
The fig tree forms its early fruit;
     the blossoming vines spread their fragrance.
Arise, come, my darling;
     my beautiful one, come with me."
(Song of Songs 2:10–13)

---

1. 4:8–12; 5:1
2. 1:9, 15; 2:2, 10, 13; 4:1, 7; 5:2; 6:4

His first recorded request is not, "Hey baby, let's get it on!" No, he asks her to go away with him, and in so doing gives her the message that he wants some time with her all to himself. He wants to be with her, away from people, pressures and interruptions, to enjoy the beauty of the spring countryside with her.

Most wives love to be alone with their husbands—especially when they know that you are just as excited about it as they are. They long to know that their company is all you need to be happy, and that you like nothing better than spending time with them. What you do is not of first importance—what is essential is that you are together. Some women are especially desirous of "quality time" with their husbands. If your wife is one of those women, and if you are a man who bears a lot of responsibility and who is easily distracted by worry, you especially need to follow the example of the husband here in the Song as he initiates to have undistracted time alone with his wife.

Let's gain additional insight into the wife's desire for companionship as she requests a romantic getaway:

> Come, my lover, let us go to the countryside,
>   let us spend the night in the villages.
> Let us go early to the vineyards
>   to see if the vines have budded,
> if their blossoms have opened,

and if the pomegranates are in bloom—
there I will give you my love.
(Song of Songs 7:11–12)

Does this sound like a boring bird-watching trip or shopping expedition? Read on. The invitation ends with her saying: "There I will give you my love." Now we're talking!

Here is how it works: in the privacy of a country retreat, your wife will be able let her worries drift away. She will be able to put aside her concerns for the kids, the house, her to-do list, her job and her friends. She will be able to relax, enjoy herself and give you herself and her body without distraction and without reserve. So are you making reservations for the bed and breakfast yet?

But let's note one other important detail: the husband, when he extended his invitation, did *not* say, as she did, "Let's go away to make love." He tactfully and wisely left that out. Are we learning anything, guys?

Your wife wants to know that she is close to you and valued by you as a person, for who she is, and not just for giving you sexual release and pleasure. Really, isn't this a more godly way to look at sex? Because the male sex drive is usually more inflammable than that of women, men must take care or we can become more focused on sex than on our friendship with our wives.

Men might have to make an effort to think about what women instinctively dwell upon. And while God purposefully designed the male gender with stronger passion, he never intended sexuality to overshadow the relationship of love and companionship.

So men, here is your wife's motto:

This is my lover, this my friend,
    O daughters of Jerusalem. (Song of Songs 5:16b)

She must have you as friend *and* lover. "Lover" alone won't cut it. Be her best friend. Then, and only then, can you also be her exciting lover.[3]

2. Confidence and Compliments

Are you ready for Love Lesson #2? Here goes:

Your wife has to feel confident about herself and her appearance before she can enjoy sex.

Love Lesson #2, corollary A:

Your opinion of your wife is the single most important human source of confidence in her life.

---

3. We have mentioned some important ways to make our wives feel loved, but we have not exhausted the subject. Study your wife and learn just what it is that makes her feel secure and special. A recommended book on coming to understand your wife's needs is *The Five Love Languages* by Gary Chapman (Chicago: Northfield Publishing, 1995).

Love Lesson #2, corollary B:

Since you, next to God, are the greatest source of confidence in your wife's life, make it your mission in life to build her up.

So where do we begin to build our wives up? Let's look at the example that the Song gives us. With his first recorded words, the husband compliments his wife, calling her "the most beautiful of women" (1:8). He thus sets the tone to which he will faithfully adhere throughout the book. He heaps praise upon her with almost every word he speaks.

Husband, let your words to your wife be full of praise, admiration and encouragement. Make her radiant with the knowledge that you think she is wonderful, great and amazing. Don't dismiss her desire for your compliments as weakness or resent it as a burden. It is the way God made her. Cooperate with his design and meet that need. When you do, she will blossom.

You really can't overdo it. Some of us think that the compliments we gave yesterday, last month or last year ought to be enough. We are like the old guy who, when his wife of many years asked him if he still loved her, replied: "I told you that I loved you when we got married. If I ever change my mind, I'll let you know!"

But exactly what are we to compliment our wives about?

He admires her voice and her face.

> Show me your face,
>   let me hear your voice;
> for your voice is sweet,
>   and your face is lovely. (Song of Songs 2:14)

He praises her appearance and her body.

> How beautiful you are, my darling!
>   Oh, how beautiful!
>   Your eyes behind your veil are doves.
> Your hair is like a flock of goats
>   descending from Mount Gilead.
> Your teeth are like a flock of sheep just shorn,
>   coming up from the washing.
> Each has its twin;
>   not one of them is alone.
> Your lips are like a scarlet ribbon;
>   your mouth is lovely.
> Your temples behind your veil
>   are like the halves of a pomegranate.
> Your neck is like the tower of David,
>   built with elegance;
> on it hang a thousand shields,
>   all of them shields of warriors.

> Your two breasts are like two fawns,
>   like twin fawns of a gazelle
>   that browse among the lilies. (Song of Songs 4:1–5)

In this, the first of three lengthy poems praising her appearance, he expresses his glowing opinion of her eyes, hair, teeth, lips, mouth, temples, neck and breasts.[4] Now, have you ever gone into that kind of detail in telling your wife how attractive she is? Try giving her some head-to-toe complimenting sessions, and watch her confidence begin to soar. Notice how he includes both her features that are seen publicly and those that he alone views in private.

It is important to express yourself specifically because your wife may not know what attracts and arouses you. She might even be surprised or a little mystified by what you like about her body, but she will be pleased to know.

He affirms her love-making.

> How delightful is your love, my sister, my bride!
>   How much more pleasing is your love than wine,
>   and the fragrance of your perfume than any spice!
> (Song of Songs 4:10)

Tell your wife how much you enjoy making love to her.

---

4. Study 6:4–7:9 to learn more about how to compliment your wife's appearance.

Tell her she is good in bed, that she is pleasing to you. If this is an area in which she needs to grow, relax and give her the time to do so. Both of you have a lifetime to learn, develop and mature as lovers. Your warm encouragement will help to give her the confidence she needs. Let her know when you have had a great night. Enlighten her about what you especially enjoyed.

The time immediately after coming together in sexual union is especially precious. Don't just roll over and drop off to sleep. Your wife has given herself to you and wants some reassurance of your love, and she wants to know that you are pleased and satisfied. An expressive, sensitive husband will find that more than likely his wife will want to be with him again and again.

Are you still a little skeptical? Check this out:

I have come into my garden, my sister, my bride;
    I have gathered my myrrh with my spice.
I have eaten my honeycomb and my honey.
(Song of Songs 5:1)

If I am reading this right, after they make love, he tells her that she was like a delectable, delicious dessert. Whew! Okay, men, the standard has been set. Loosen up, don't be shy—don't hold back; say it!

He praises her extravagantly.

> All beautiful you are, my darling;
>   there is no flaw in you. (Song of Songs 4:7)

He says she is "all beautiful" and flawless. Come on, isn't he going over the top? Obviously, no woman—or man, for that matter—is perfect!

We have a vital lesson to learn here: *Your wife will move in the direction of your words.* Are they words of compliment or criticism? What do you talk about—her attractive features, or her blemishes, imperfections and defects?

Men, many of us must confess that we often say little to compliment our wife's appearance. Rarely do we initiate; she usually has to ask. "How do I look?" she inquires, and we answer with a muttered, "Okay," or "You look fine." Your wife will probably not be excited about making love to you with "compliments" like these!

Criticism doesn't work, either. Most women are already insecure and critical of their appearance. If your wife gets the slightest hint that you are not pleased with the way she looks, she will feel unattractive and might struggle with having confidence. Sadly, too many of us behave as if our nit-picking and fault-finding could embarrass our wives into being more beautiful and sexy. We think by comparing her unfavorably to a movie star, a supermodel or some other woman, we will shame her into becoming the raving vixen that we think she should be. Not only do these strategies not work, they have the opposite effect. When we disapprove of our wives, especially in the highly sensitive areas of appearance and sexual performance, we discourage them, and their ability to respond sexually goes right out the window.

Think about it—there is not *one word* of criticism uttered by the husband in the Song. Are we on to something? You better believe it. With this kind of a positive atmosphere, is it any mystery why the story of their marriage is laced with so many delicious sexual encounters? Don't all of us want the same kind of intimacy? Let's start praising our wives. They need it, they love it, and they deserve it.

3. Charming, Courteous and Considerate

Sexual love is like a flower: beautiful and desirable, but delicate and elusive. Lots of other things in the system of the plant need to be working for that flower to appear. The least disturbance in the soil, the stem, the branches and the leaves can inhibit or prevent the blossom from coming to life. Men, wise up and pay attention to the whole system; don't just focus on the flower.

Sex for men can be more like a cash crop than a delicate flower. We figure that if we plow, sow and pray for rain, we'll get a harvest. Well, if you want a sex life that compares to a field of corn or barley, keep thinking like that. If, on the other hand, you want to see the blossoming of your wife's desire, you will have to learn another way.

Sex for women is about subtlety, nuance and delicacy. Blessed is the man who learns to be charming, courteous and considerate, and blessed is his wife and marriage. Let's learn to do the things that set the stage for great sex.

Take her out to eat.

> He has taken me to the banquet hall,
>   and his banner over me is love.
> Strengthen me with raisins,
>   refresh me with apples,
>   for I am faint with love. (Song of Songs 2:4–5)

Food may be sustenance to you, but for women, the right meal in the right atmosphere is romantic. Where does she like to go out to eat? Take her there. Plan it yourself; don't always make her ask. Take her out to a special place for dessert. If you have time constraints, just stop on the way home and pick up that sugary treat. Certainly, friend, your motives in this are selfless, sincere and loving, but what man in his right mind, if his wife offered, would turn down a second course of "dessert" later on that evening?

Realize the power of a word 'aptly spoken' (Proverbs 25:11).

How we say things is important. The right words open the door of our wife's desires, the wrong ones can slam it shut. Check out how our hero in the Song expresses himself—he has a way with a winsome and attractive phrase. Just for starters he calls her eyes "doves." He says her breasts are "the twin fawns of a gazelle" and her lips are a "scarlet ribbon" (see 4:1–7). Reread the Song, noting carefully what he said and how he said it. No, you don't have to become a poet or use the exact words this man did, but, my friend, you have got to learn to be romantic, flirtatious, subtle and tactfully indirect as you talk to your wife about sex.

Here is how it goes for some of us:

We silently get in bed and grope, hoping for the best.

We use vulgar slang terms that cheapen sex and

make our wives feel dirty.

We are painfully blunt: "It's been a long time. Let's have sex."

Still others of us use medical terms: "Your anatomy is awakening my libido. May we copulate tonight?"

Surely we can do better than this!

To become charming lovers, we need to look at some verses we have referred to already, but that are so crucial as to merit further attention. We will divide up the following passage to clearly identify which of the lovers is speaking. Note carefully the progression of conversation and events:

Lover [the husband]
    You are a garden locked up, my sister, my bride;
        you are a spring enclosed, a sealed fountain.
    Your plants are an orchard of pomegranates
        with choice fruits,
        with henna and nard,
        nard and saffron,
        calamus and cinnamon,
        with every kind of incense tree,
        with myrrh and aloes
        and all the finest spices.
    You are a garden fountain,

a well of flowing water
streaming down from Lebanon.
(Song of Songs 4:12–15)

How and when a husband says things to his wife is
vitally important in sexual love. The wrong words at the
wrong time spell disaster and have ruined many a night.
In the passage above, the husband notes that his wife
is "a garden locked up." (Recall that the wife's "garden"
is a poetic reference to her most intimate sexual areas.)
He expresses how attractive and beautiful her garden is
to him. Interestingly, he calls it her garden, even though
in marriage her body totally belongs to him (as does his
to her). If he were like some of us he would say,
"Unlock that garden and let me in! I am your husband
and it belongs to me." Thankfully, he is wiser and more
loving than that. Instead, he compliments her beauty.
He charms, woos and wins her. He respects her bodily
privacy and honors her with rightful dignity.

What happens next speaks volumes about the way
our wives respond when they are treated with chivalry.
The wife warms to her husband. She freely, willingly
and eagerly opens her "garden" for him to enter, taste
and possess. Listen to her invitation:

Beloved [the wife]
    Awake, north wind,

and come, south wind!
Blow on my garden,
    that its fragrance may spread abroad.
Let my lover come into his garden
    and taste its choice fruits. (Song of Songs 4:16)

So, husbands, lesson learned? Good! Let's leave this section with a happy man's testimony to a night well spent:

I have come into my garden, my sister, my bride;
    I have gathered my myrrh with my spice.
I have eaten my honeycomb and my honey;
    I have drunk my wine and my milk.
(Song of Songs 5:1)

4. Charisma of Cleanliness

Let's introduce this section with a series of verses spoken by the wife. As you read, give special attention to the italicized words, and ask yourself if your wife could say these things about you.

Let him kiss me with the kisses of his mouth—
    for your love is more delightful than wine.
Pleasing is the fragrance of your perfumes;
    your name is like perfume poured out.
    No wonder the maidens love you!
(Song of Songs 1:2–3, emphasis mine)

Like an apple tree among the trees of the forest
   is my lover among the young men.
I delight to sit in his shade,
   and *his fruit is sweet to my taste.*
(Song of Songs 2:3, emphasis mine)

Who is this coming up from the desert
   like a column of smoke,
perfumed with myrrh and incense
   made from all the spices of the merchant?
Look! It is Solomon's carriage.
(Song of Songs 3:6–7, emphasis mine)

My lover is radiant and ruddy,
   outstanding among ten thousand.
His head is purest gold;
   his hair is wavy
   and black as a raven.
His eyes are like doves
   by the water streams,
washed in milk,
   mounted like jewels.
His cheeks are like beds of spice
   yielding perfume.
His lips are like lilies
   dripping with myrrh.
His arms are rods of gold
   set with chrysolite.
His body is like polished ivory
   decorated with sapphires.

His legs are pillars of marble
    set on bases of pure gold.
His appearance is like Lebanon,
choice as its cedars.
    His mouth is sweetness itself;
    he is altogether lovely.
    This is my lover, this my friend,
O daughters of Jerusalem.
(Song of Songs 5:10–16, emphasis mine)

Husbands, if you want a great love life, make yourself desirable. If you are offensive to her senses, don't expect your wife to summon you to her bed. Respect her enough to shower, shave and use cologne. Brush and floss, and use mouthwash. Get rid of the locker-room behavior that preteen boys find so amusing, but women find insulting. And don't just do these things when you are "in the mood"—make them a habit.

Don't dismiss good grooming, attention to appearance, the practice of hygiene, and the use of cologne as the surefire signs of the dandified, pompous man. Nor should we regard concern with cleanliness and hygiene as a frivolous luxury or a concession to feminine quirkiness. No, these practices are the habits of a good husband and a gentleman. I get the sense that the guy in the Song was no wimpy weakling—rather, he was confident, masculine and virile. Let's learn from him, imitate him, and have the great love life with our wives that he had with his.

Let your wife help you choose a cologne that you both like, and start using it daily. You might even come to have your own signature fragrance! Your wife will get used to the scent, and its lingering essence will bring you to her mind even when you are absent. Your kids will mention it—positively. My dad was a blue-collar "man's man" who managed a large semi-trailer truck operation. Even though he didn't dress in a three-piece suit to go to work, he always looked good and smelled great. I still remember the familiar fragrance of his Old Spice shaving lotion and Vitalis hair tonic. It surrounded him with a distinctive aroma, and gave me a sense of his strong, masculine presence.

In my younger years, my three older sisters taught me a lot about how to treat women and how to be a gentleman. (And may I say, with the full intent of sounding "Old School," I don't think we are teaching our young men much about manners these days.) They taught me two basic fashion lessons: 1) look neat and 2) wear what looks good on you. They taught me that when walking with a woman, the man walks next to the street and *always* opens the door for the lady. I learned the walking and door-opening lessons so well that I have on several occasions nearly broken a leg while maneuvering to get in the proper position!

Find out what your wife likes you to wear. Let her help you shop for some clothes that enhance your appearance. Learn what fashions make you look your best, and dress accordingly. Develop your own style that suits your physique, personality, pocketbook and age. You will discover that care and concern for your everyday attire will make quite a difference in how your wife feels about you. Who says a little attention to our wardrobe won't help give us a little extra sexual charisma at home?

Men, may we become the sensitive, strong and sensual husbands we need to be. Are you with me? Let's work at it. Our wives will thank us, and we...umm... (how do I say it tactfully?)...Let me just say that we will *get to enjoy a lot more time in the garden!*

Afterword

Daughters of Jerusalem, I charge you
   by the gazelles and by the does of the field:
Do not arouse or awaken love until it so desires.
Song of Songs 2:7

Writing about an area as sensitive and personal as sexual intimacy in marriage is a delicate and difficult task. It is easy to be misunderstood, and easy to misunderstand. In the introduction and throughout the book I have attempted to address the difficult or exceptional circumstance, and have tried to leave room for couples to take what they read and apply it as they think best in their own marriage.

I am putting pen to paper to say this one more time. Let me leave you with a few thoughts as we conclude. These may be some of the most important to take with you, aside from the teaching on the five senses themselves.

How to Respond

Let this book be an informative and enlightening

source to inspire you to think more biblically about sex and sexuality in your marriage. Let it be for you a pathway to greater freedom, confidence and joy. But don't, as we said in the introduction, put pressure on yourself or your spouse—that will backfire, for sure.

Do not be discouraged, depressed or defeated as you see the ideal sexual relationship, which we have considered in studying the Song. One part of the Song that we did not cover (5:6–8) tells of a time of separation and disappointment for the couple in the story. Every marriage has those times, and sexual difficulties and arguments can be among the most volatile and confusing that we face. Have you had arguments and frustrations in your sexual relationship in marriage? Well then, join the rest of us!

In all of my years of counseling married couples, I have never met a couple who had an idyllic, perfect sex life. The reason is found in the very nature of sexual intimacy. In perhaps no other area of our relationship are we more open to being embarrassed, disappointed and insecure. Is it any wonder that there are times of difficulty?

Some of us carry memories from painful past experiences that haunt us still. We may have been abused, or we may have abused. We may have been careless or ignorant in our earlier years, and we have the scars to prove it. We may have experienced a failed marriage, or felt the pain of unfaithfulness in our present one.

Some of these experiences and memories thankfully fade into the background as we discover God's plan and build a life based upon it, and upon marital love and faithfulness. But even so, we must realize we are imperfect people in a fallen world, and that as long as we are here we will feel the sense of incompleteness and struggle that being in this world brings to us all.

Others of us may read the book, and be ready to launch out boldly. Be careful not to overwhelm your partner, who may not be quite as ready for radical change. Let's give each other the time we need. Let's be patient—on both sides of that continuum. A friend told me recently of reading that a marriage should be the playground of God's grace. Extend freely to each other the grace God has extended to you in Christ.

Usually in a marriage, one partner is more aggressive and adventurous, and the other more passive and timid. There is not a right or a wrong here, but there is a need for love and consideration. If we are more concerned to please than to be pleased, to build up than to be built up, then we will come to a better place together.

A Lifetime to Grow

Sexual intimacy is an area in which we grow, not a destination at which we arrive. Enjoy growing together. One of the greatest testaments to the wisdom of God in reserving sexual intimacy for those in relationships committed for life is that he knows we will need an unhurried span in which to grow sexually, just as in every other area. When a married couple has a bad encounter in lovemaking, all is not lost! You'll still be married and in love tomorrow, and you can keep learning and growing.

If you have had or are having a period of difficulty sexually, take heart! You, with God's power and wisdom, can overcome and you will probably be amazed at the oneness that comes as you find victories together. It may take time, prayer and some godly counsel, but there are effective tools God has provided for your assistance.

If you are experiencing illness or other hindrances to an ideal sexual life, and feel limited in what is available to you in sexual expression, be thankful for what you do have, and enjoy it to the full. Remember, too, that you indeed did commit to each other "in sickness and in health." Your marriage was not and is not founded upon sex, but upon a loving commitment to your partner "for better or for worse." Sex is a way—a great way—to be close and to express love, but it is not the be-all and end-all of your marriage.

For those of us who are experiencing the changes that children, middle age and aging in general bring to our romantic life, we need to realize that change is not to be dreaded, but embraced. At each stage of our life, with our differing responsibilities and health conditions, our sexual responsiveness and relationship will evolve. But let us not allow it to diminish or founder. Let it change and re-form graciously, as we all the while maintain an appropriate intimacy and passion for the stage of life in which we find ourselves.

Of course, nothing will destroy the beauty of marital love as God planned it more than sin, and especially sexual sin. The joys we have described in this book cannot be found by those who seek pleasure in pornography, self-gratification or extra-marital affairs. Such behavior is not just an epidemic in our world; it has infected many in our churches as well. Unless there is radical repentance here, many will have no chance of finding sexual intimacy and joy in their marriages. If you are feeling alone, defeated and hopeless, there is help available through many avenues. This is the subject of other good books which I urge you to read where needed.

I am sure we have a few doubters and cynics

among our readers. Yet, if you are still reading, something kept you going this far. If you are still a bit scornful and incredulous, I encourage you to think again, and to reconsider. One of the places to which we retreat when we have been disappointed is to the refuge of pessimism and skepticism. I have gone there on various issues from time to time in my life, and I can only share with you that I have never liked the guy I turned out to be as a result.

Give what you read in here a chance—a big chance, for a period of time. My conviction is that as you and your spouse grow in your expressiveness in the five senses of romantic love, your marriage will be happier, closer and more fulfilled than ever before.

Perhaps the best way to close our thoughts is with the pledge of love and the call to the lover to come and make love...for we have seen throughout the Song how our loving devotion leads to a joyful sexual union.

> Place me like a seal over your heart,
>   like a seal on your arm;
> for love is as strong as death,
>   its jealousy unyielding as the grave.
> It burns like blazing fire,

like a mighty flame.
Many waters cannot quench love;
   rivers cannot wash it away.
If one were to give all the wealth of his house for love,
   it would be utterly scorned....
You who dwell in the gardens
   with friends in attendance,
   let me hear your voice!
Come away, my lover,
   and be like a gazelle
or like a young stag
   on the spice-laden mountains.
(Song of Songs 8:6–7, 13–14)

Bibliography

Carr, G. Lloyd. *The Song of Solomon: Tyndale Old Testament Commentaries.* Ed. D. J. Wiseman. Downers Grove, IL: InterVarsity Press, 1984.

Dillow, Joseph C. *Solomon on Sex.* Nashville: Thomas Nelson Publishers, 1977.

Dillow, Linda and Lorraine Pintus. *Intimate Issues: 24 Questions Christian Women Ask About Sex.* Colorado Springs: Waterbrook Press, 1999.

Chapman, Gary. *The Five Love Languages.* Chicago: Northfield Publishing, 1995.

LaHaye, Tim and Beverly. *The Act of Marriage: The Beauty of Sexual Love.* Grand Rapids: Zondervan, 1998.

LaHaye, Tim and Beverly. *The Act of Marriage after 40: Making Love for Life.* Grand Rapids: Zondervan, 2000.

Laing, Sam and Geri. *Friends and Lovers.* Spring Hill, TN: DPI, 1996.

Longman, Tremper, III. *Song of Songs: New International Commentary on the Old Testament.* Ed. Robert Hubbard. Grand Rapids: Eerdmans, 2001.

Sakenfeld, Katharine, Ed. *The Interpreter's Dictionary of the Bible.* Nashville: Abingdon Press, 1962.

Friends and Lovers

Friendship and romantic love are the two essential ingredients of a great marriage, the qualities that will make it grow ever richer, deeper and more fulfilling. The Laings encourage you to put aside your preconceptions, your problems and your past. Above all, get rid of your low expectations. A marriage relationship between two people who are friends and lovers is not just for the gifted, the beautiful or the few. It is intended for everyone, including you.

Be Still, My Soul

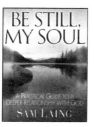

In twenty-two short but poignant chapters, Sam Laing shows how we can all walk with God, enjoy God and have an intimate fellowship with him that gets better with the passing of time. Sharing from his life, from his heart and from the Scriptures, Sam shows us the essence of the spiritual life. Here is a book you will return to again and again when your soul yearns for God.

The Guilty Soul's Guide to Grace

Writing from the fresh perspective of an avowed "Guilty Soul," Sam Laing shares openly from his life experiences and from the Scriptures about the need for Christians to grasp the often unclaimed gift of God's grace. Sam says, "What are you waiting for? Take off the chains that Jesus died to free you from. Realize that it is for freedom that Christ has set you free."

Mighty Man of God:

Believing that the condition of manhood in our world is deplorable and that the masculine gender is viewed as superficial and foolish, Sam Laing calls men to ascend to the heights of nobility that God intended. He calls them to forsake the paths of selfishness and vulgarity and become heroes who think of themselves last and others first. He assures them that they can conquer their weaknesses and fears and can forge onward and upward to their true destiny—to become mighty men of God!

Raising Awesome Kids in Troubled Times

Experienced parents and speakers for family seminars, Sam and Geri Laing offer real, everyday answers to the questions raised by parents seeking to be the best influence in their children's lives. Drawing from their own experiences with their four children, the Laings offer in-depth help for parents while laying a biblical framework upon which to build a strong family.

The Wonder Years

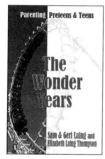

Enjoy the ride of your life—the wonder years. Raising preteens and teens is a wild, crazy roller-coaster ride. Hold on to your seat while Sam and Geri—and married daughter, Elizabeth—give godly guidance to help you navigate these challenging but exhilarating years. Written from the perspective of both parent and child, this book will help you to understand, communicate with and guide your children through these tumultuous years to accountable adulthood.